All Creation Works Together

To Bless the Earth and Humankind with Bountiful Life

by

Fr. Raymond Kirtz O.M.I.

DORRANCE
PUBLISHING CO
EST. 1920
PITTSBURGH, PENNSYLVANIA 15238

Dorrance Publishing Co
585 Alpha Drive
Suite 103
Pittsburgh, PA 15238
Visit our website at www.dorrancebookstore.com

ISBN: 978-1-4809-1212-0
eISBN: 978-1-4809-1543-3

Contents

Preface

This book is all about Creation. While based on contemporary astrophysics, as well as the Genesis story of Creation, it is neither detailed cosmology nor Scriptural exegesis. The book begins with a preamble reflecting on Jesus of Nazareth, the risen Lord, as a model and exemplar for understanding our place in Creation. The first chapter that follows, "God Writes Cosmicwide," suggests that it is important to give attention to the universe and more specifically to the earth we inhabit because our faith relationship with the Creator and the quality of life on this earth depend a lot on how we view our relationship to the universe and the earth. The understanding of the universe as envisioned by earliest humankind, including the peoples described in the Old Testament, dovetail with the theories of contemporary science. They do not contradict one another because those older traditions sought the meaning of their existence within the cosmos they could observe, while contemporary science seeks physical details. Those earlier observations, though obviously scientifically deficient, provided those people with valuable insights into their relationship to the universe and to the Creator.

They gained their wisdom to live on this earth through their simple eye contact with the earth and the surrounding universe as seen in the night sky. While we moderns have devised ways to live more comfortably and securely within our earthen environment, we are in dire need of the wisdom of those ancients that would help us use our advanced technologies without destroying the earth and our environment. More specifically, we need the wisdom to inhabit the earth in such a way that our lives are a ministry benefiting the earth, and so the earth can minister to us as the Creator clearly intended it to be.

The chapters on the seven Sacraments of the Church deal almost entirely with the physical matter of those Sacraments and their Earth and Creation foundations, much as the Hebrew Old Covenant practices were so based. The purpose is to illustrate how the material matter of each Sacrament exhibits a particular ministry of the Risen Lord manifested through natural elements of Creation.

The chapter on the Beatitudes is intended to reflect on the Kingdom of Heaven as highlighted in the Beatitudes of Jesus. Jesus proclaims that this Kingdom is our heritage intended for the restoration of the original condition of Creation disrupted through sin. The Beatitudes do not detail obligations as much as the gifts of Creation.

The chapter on Mary, the mother of Jesus, highlights her unique role in the Creator's Creation/Salvation process. At the birth of her son Jesus, angels from the realm of the Creator proclaimed her full of Creation's Graces. Through her response to the call of the Creator, Mary became a vital contributor to the long anticipated fullness of Creation/Redemption. Mary never taught science or theology, but she gave us her son Jesus, the Word of God, the same Word that was present throughout Creation's beginnings and ongoing processes.

The next four chapters are a wrap-up of all these reflections, including reflection on the Christmas Star and the place of the Church in this scheme of Creation. Devoid of a specific sense of its place in Creation, the Church flounders in its attempts to draw new members to join and to keep existing members from leaving. If the Church does not clearly see itself as having a place in the scheme of Creation, it will be perceived as irrelevant to the world. As some say it, everything functions in the economy of Creation.

A final chapter on extraterrestrials is not a science fiction distraction. Based on the growing conviction in the scientific community of the probability of other life forms in the universe, it is suggested that we do ourselves a greater service if we anticipate beneficial outcomes from possible encounters with aliens rather than the seeming conviction that aliens will always be dangerous and ugly. If we think that way, we reinforce our own tendencies to lethal reactions. No matter where civilizations might exist, they have all gotten their existence from the same loving Creator. Besides, we may never meet.

But first: the preamble that precedes those chapters will be a nontheological reflection on Jesus of the Gospels as the one who can help us appreciate the place of humankind in the chronicle of Creation. He is the quintessence, the crowning glory of Creation, but fully in consonance with the human condition. For that reason, this book begins with Jesus of Nazareth. The place of his birth was the site of an animal stable with animals present, especially sheep brought in by shepherds, all of which put this family and newborn child in touch with raw natural Creation. Those details of the Gospel story seem to establish the fact that the Creator intended to accomplish the Redemption of humankind within the down-to-earth situation of human life within Creation, and to give the assurance that the Divine intervention would not be overwhelming to humankind but would be affirming of the human condition in spite of human sin.

Culturally, Jesus grew up with a sense of Creation—and it was Creation, not just nature. The Aramaic people sensed the reality of Creation, and knew the Creator from that Creation. They interacted with the Creator through created things, seasons, and especially growing things. From all this, Jesus absorbed the Spirituality and natural touch that made him such a powerful teacher.

All the chapters following the preamble are intended to put us in touch with that same Creation we today only know through science and education and our limited contacts with outdoor nature. The hope is you will be able to imagine and perceive Creation as Jesus intuitively lived it within his culture, within the confines of the cosmos he saw in the sky above. This is not so much a teaching book as it is a reflection to enlarge our vision and Creation-enriched sensitivities to prepare ourselves for a future that most forecasters predict will be very different from what we have known. Our best bet will be to become more Creation minded than we have been accustomed to. Only such a frame of mind will give us the incentives needed to make the necessary changes to our earth-destroying way of life so the future of humankind and the earth will be more promising.

Preamble: Jesus, Paragon of Creation

All stories have a timeline and characters. I begin this story of Creation with Jesus of Nazareth, even though his timeline includes only a very short span of the timeline of Creation. Even that pivotal event of his death on a Cross really cannot be appreciated in its full reality unless we see it in the context of Creation. Redemption itself is Creation centered because humankind is Creation enveloped and is Graced with Redemption through the medium of Creation. The journey of Jesus to his Cross was an earthen journey.

When Jesus was dying on that Cross, humanly speaking he was as low as any human could ever be. He was helpless; his end was in sight. Yet when the thief dying on his own cross next to Jesus said, "Remember me when you come into your power," Jesus gave a reply that might seem to have been otherworldly: "I promise that today you will be with me in Paradise." Yet Jesus was not exercising Divine, otherworldly knowledge. Dying on that Cross, Jesus was experiencing the fullness of his life as he had never experienced it before.

What he was experiencing was not just suffering and death, but Creation itself being renewed. We can never understand the burden of that. He was on the threshold of his earthly life and his entry into his Kingdom at the right hand of the Father. While still in this life he cried out in a dreadful sense of loss: "My God, why have you forsaken me?" For a moment, sin seemed to have won over everything good in the world, and all Creation itself hung in the balance. At that moment it seemed like loss, yet inspired by his closeness to the Father, there is a depth of comprehension of the reality of the moment that far exceeded what he would have been able to muster under less significant circumstances.

Through all that, he was able to express almost unbelievable forgiveness, forgiving the sin of his tormentors: "Father, forgive them……" Through that forgiving act all sin is being forgiven and redeemed. Perhaps carried along with the Grace of the moment, the criminal dying next to Jesus rebuked the other criminal who had taunted Jesus and now affirms Jesus: "Unlike us who deserve our punishment, you have done nothing wrong. Remember me..." And Jesus replied: "This day you will be with me in Paradise." That thief represented every one of us who are also struggling between sin and vital choices for the good, also with Jesus beside us.

Let us explore the Creational context of that moment. All three crosses, standing there on the hill called Golgotha, are planted in the soil of the earth which represents all Creation which has been wounded by ages of accumulated sin and evil. The terrible battle between evil and good rages within and around those three unlikely companions in suffering. The two thieves and the earth, along with all Creation that encompasses them are all lifted up to an unbelievable new and invigorating life accruing from the death of Jesus of Nazareth.

The universe that rejoiced at the announcement of the birth of the long-awaited Messiah now trembles in every bit of itself, whether it be the gargantuan stars and galaxies or the tiniest bits of it, all tremble as a cry escapes from the mouth of Jesus as he is at the threshold of his Kingdom, a cry that resounds not only in the ears of the women at the foot of the Cross and the Roman executioners and the few by-standers, but resonates all throughout the universe: "It is finished!" At that moment, Jesus has accomplished the Creation-wide work that had begun at his birth in Bethlehem of Judea.

Charles Dickens wrote in the beginning of his great story, *A Tale of Two Cities*: "It was the worst of times and the best of times..." That is the way the story of the Crucifixion could have been told. Only then, the worst and the best are exponentially greater. The worst of times! All history, and all humankind are in the equation here and evil has seemingly conquered the One who is the source of all good. Nonetheless, the best of times; Salvation history is coming to completion, though he is dying. It is over for him, the one who had carried the hopes of so many seemed to have failed. The Romans thought so. The Temple authorities thought so. Even the disciples of Jesus thought so. Yet the Father of Jesus and the Father of us all knew otherwise. It is the best of times.

There is something coming about that is beyond human comprehension. What is transpiring here is of cosmic proportions. Jesus the Victim, in his humanity is bringing all cosmic reality to healing. All Creation is renewed. The fulfillment of human Redemption foreseen by the Creator as inevitable since the creation of humankind gifted with freedom to choose evil has come to completion. Evil had been chosen, over and over again, yet the created good in humankind had not been destroyed.

One momentous and redeeming choice of good had been accomplished there on that ignominious Cross, a choice Jesus was free to make or refuse. In full human freedom he went against the grain and chose the Redeeming good. What is transpiring there at that Crucifixion moment is of all-history and Creation-encompassing proportions. In the depth of his being, Jesus is in tune with all that. His whole being must have been drumming with the surge of Creation's first beginning and its eons-long evolution. The best of times.

That moment and that deed forecast future potentials of love emanating from humankind that we could never have believed possible. Jesus is the sublime exemplar of Creation and human potential. Through him we are assured that Creation still has potentials not yet fulfilled. It is the living presence of the risen Lord that gives us the assurance of our potentials we cannot even imagine.

In the recent past we have heard about a so-called Human Potential Movement. This refers to a psychologically designed program intended to help people become more confident and active in achieving their best. That no doubt has been productive of some good one can hope, yet such a human potential movement pales in efforts and results compared to what God still wants to do for his beloved humankind.

Jesus thought in a much grander scale. He knew God has something even grander in mind than what we have ever imagined or could express. Jesus always saw beyond simple human potential that we might have in mind. This was encapsulated in his teaching about the Kingdom of God which will be dealt with in a following chapter (Chapter 12, The Kingdom of the Beatitudes).

The very physical cosmos beckons humankind to the Creator, the source of all our human potentials. To reach that goal depends on recognizing that our full potential resides in God-like love. That is the greatest facet of our Divine image. God loves momentously and God sees momentous possibilities for our love also. The awesome act of Creating was an expression of the love of the Creator; and grand things for ongoing Creation can come about through the love of humankind.

Our place in Creation is not only to build bigger and better machines to traverse the galaxy or the universe, though we do seem to be called to just that. However, those accomplishments are going to need an overarching value, a value our culture presently does not provide very well. In our Western culture, our goal is to travel, dominate, and get everything we can from the new place for our own benefit. We seem to not be able to get beyond our self-serving intentions believing that serves us best.

The Creator has gifted us with potential far beyond the physical and intellectual. Our destiny to one day live in a more intimate presence of the Divine predisposes us to gifts and energies (Graces) we do not seem to appreciate.

We seem only to be able to speak of *doing* something, and only with difficulty do we comprehend a new sense of *being*. The famous playwright Shakespeare, in his play *Hamlet*, delved into the question "To be or not to be?" At least he recognized *that* as the ultimate problem, though I will not follow his character Hamlet all the way in his rumination: "To be or not to be; that is the question; Whether 'tis nobler in the mind to suffer the stings and arrows of outrageous fortune, Or to take arms against a sea of troubles." It is typically human to take up arms. We need to get beyond Shakespeare and get to matters that may not have occurred to us or Shakespeare.

Not too long ago a national political campaign became famous for a four-word statement of one of the candidates: "It's the economy, stupid!" To cash in on that gimmick with a three-word acclamation that also says it all: "It's Creation, stupid!" It would have been preferred to leave off the "stupid" word, except we are all afflicted with the same lack of understanding about the more profound whys and wherefores of all things political, economic, and all else. We fail to appreciate that everything fits into the scheme of Creation. Never do most of us give consideration to this, but if we did, we would for sure find more answers to our difficulties than we find from our usual sources.

The Creator was confident in gifting humankind with freedom, knowing that not only what would be our propensity toward evil, but also our implanted capacity for healing from the wounds of sin. Physical earth grows from the brute forces of earthquakes, volcanoes, floods, and erosions, and is also self-healing from those same events. Humankind has an even greater predisposition to healing from the brutality of sin.

Contrary to the processes of physical nature that are totally random and haphazard, our growth to ever greater fullness is a gradual but sure process freely chosen. All this bares the motif, the evident markings of the love of the Creator himself. This is Creation at its best. From all these considerations, we can enjoy the confidence that we are capable of a better future than we sometimes fear is possible.

We will now continue with a very short narration of this Creation/cosmos story and with reflections on their import for our lives now and for the future of humankind. We can find reasons for optimism and incentives for making changes in how we live out our share of this Creation story. We live in neither the worst of times nor the best of times, but in a very crucial time in the history of Creation. So then, to begin, what can we learn from the story of Creation, and why should we care about all that?

1
God Writes Cosmicwide

One of the first things most of us learn as growing infants is how many feet we have, or maybe how many ears we have. Soon enough, under parental prodding, we are able to say two. For a while, it will make not the least bit of difference how many feet or ears we have; it is just one of those fun things parents do with us. However, we are learning. The child will always want to know more, and never would any elder try to keep a child from learning. Who would think it good to keep a child from seeing, hearing, feeling, smelling the out of doors?

Yet, there are some who seem to question the value of exploring the universe beyond the earth to learn more about what is out there. The attitude among some seems to be, we know there is a God who created it, so why do we need to know any more? It is so far out of sight, what value can there be in knowing anymore? But that would be like a child saying to parents, I know you gave me life, but I don't want to know any more about you or about our world. Think of the horrible relationship that would develop between parents and children. Children would not know or appreciate parents, and much of what we call human social life would disintegrate because we do not know how to relate.

Think now what such an attitude does to our faith relationship with the Creator; "I know everything I need to know about you and your Creation. It is too fearful to know any more." Faith life would be very weak and ineffectual. On the other hand, think of the intimacy with the Creator we can experience if we eagerly seek to expand our knowledge and appreciation of Creation as an avenue to knowing the Creator. An earnest scientist finds joy in expanding his knowledge for science's sake, whereas a believer finds satisfaction in getting to know the Creator. One's image of the Creator will expand and become more meaningful with more knowledge of the universe. A believer who is satisfied with archaic, uninteresting images of the Divine that are less inspiring than images of the universe that science is providing us today will not be moved to a wholehearted faith, if they continue to believe at all.

It is not enough to know that God is all-knowing, that God made all things, that God will last forever, that God had no beginning and will have no end. Just knowing this in our heads will not help to either transform our lives or inspire another to faith. Until we get to know and are profoundly moved by a sense of the Creator that stretches our minds and emotions to their limits, the benefits of science and technology will more strongly grab our attention and motivate our strongest efforts, and give us our greatest satisfaction. Then we might follow those who say: Who needs God?

The God who is mirrored in a little garden patch is truly a beautiful God, but the image of that God can be augmented by an enlarged view of the garden of the universe. We need both gardens to come to know the full wonder of the Creator. As believers discover more of Creation that science is uncovering for us, our image of God will certainly expand. God beckons to believers from the depths of our sciences, though that may not be true for the atheist scientist who cannot discover anything spiritual in physical science. For people of faith, our God who created and reigns over such an awe-inspiring universe will draw us ever more closely into his enlivening presence.

God definitely intends us to appreciate not only this mind-boggling universe, but also, and just as importantly, to appreciate that we are created in the image of such a wise, providential God. Our minds and hearts can expand to their full potential as we ponder the wonder of this universe and the wonder of ourselves. The Creator has designed us to function in unison with the universe and the earth as Creation comes to fullness.

A mind not regulated by faith can run dangerously wild, but a mind regulated by faith is God's gift to Creation. Faith does not need science, but science, the product of our God-given gifts, can enrich faith. It would be a lame excuse on our part to say that ancient people, including the Old Testament people, did not need all our science for their faith to thrive and grow, so why do we need scientific knowledge to enhance our faith? We need to grow in knowledge because scientific knowledge is an indispensable part of who we are today.

Most of us who live in this contemporary scientific world cannot put science and technology aside like the Amish and other more conservative folks like them do because they have chosen a simpler life style; but who can deny that their archaic faith-inspired values are much to be admired? Our more contemporary lifestyles, even with all the scientific advances, are fine too as long as we learn how to live in ways that are not destructive to the earth and to ourselves.

However, the quality of life for future generations will not be improved if all we have is scientific knowledge to pass on. Without faith, they will have to struggle with even more destructive tendencies than we are dealing with today, and it could become disastrously more dangerous on this earth. Future generations as well as we today need an enlightened scientific enterprise moderated by a dynamic, life-enhancing faith. Our faith-inspired sense of God and a Spirituality based on that image can grow proportionately with our scientific knowledge, and with such a faith-enriched culture, we can avoid worshiping our sciences as we tend do today with the attending bad results.

We today seem to be in about the same predicament as the builders of the Tower of Babel mentioned in Genesis 11, 1-9, who said to one another: "Come let us build ourselves a city and a tower with its top in the sky, and so make a name for ourselves.... [T]he Lord came down to see the city and the tower that the men had built.... [T]he Lord scattered them from there all over the earth, and they *stopped building the tower...that came to be called Babel*" (Gen 11, 1-9). The author of Genesis seems to say they learned their lesson and stopped building that tower and grew Spiritually more mature.

We moderns need to recognize that the Lord "has also come down to us" with admonitions concerning our own works. We have the capability of reading the Divine message suitable to our situation; we too have immature goals for ourselves. It is all right for us to reach beyond the heavens—the reaches of the earth—and on out into the far reaches of the cosmos, because out there we will find the script the Creator is writing for us today. We can grow Spiritually more mature as we recognize the majestic wonder of that Creator and the actual smallness of ourselves. A big arrogant head will not get us as far as we can go, but a humble heart will imitate the humility of the Creator himself who allows us to explore his creation to its limits. The Creator does not hold us back from those efforts as long as we do not lose sight of our ultimate goal: ever-greater union with the Creator, bringing Creation along the path to fullness. It is our privilege to share in that process with the special "image" gifts the Creator has shared with us.

2

There Is an Appointed Time
for Everything in the Creation Process

Now in imagination we will launch out into the universe and reflect on the scenario of Creation's beginnings and ongoing development. The well-known passage from the Biblical book Ecclesiastes that many may be familiar with— "There is an appointed Time for Everything" (Eccl 3, 1-11)—will set the tone for a condensed time journey. These next couple chapters will be both scientific and Biblical in their foundations, but will be neither detailed scientific nor Biblical explanations.

Most of us may remember listening to the renowned physicist Carl Sagan expound more exactly and more colorfully on these matters on television science shows, and who introduced the unscientific term "stuff" to name so much of what he was talking about. Other resources can be found on the internet and libraries, including Brian Swimme, who wrote *The Epic Story of Cosmic, Earth and Human Transformation*. He and others describe in more detail what I am going to be gliding over, and who has not marveled at the many, many photos taken by the Hubble telescope circling the earth high above us showing photographic evidence of those first physical processes? Based on all that evidence, and on the common faith in a Divine Creator that many of us share, I continue my narrative.

Before time or any material existed, God created the first minute matter that became our universe. In the very beginning there was a period of time, perhaps microseconds, for all those basic elements and particles to assemble together to form new elements. Through a process lasting billions upon billions of years, there was, as though it were in the Creator's timetable, time for

4

that material hot from Creation's first beginning explosion to cool down and continue its process of forming that universe we see about us. There was a time for those elements to form solid pieces of matter, and for those small pieces to form into larger bodies, the stars. It was a time of much banging together and breaking asunder, all of a magnitude that no living being could have witnessed and survived.

There was a time for those stars to begin moving about with everything held in place by a special feature of this conglomeration called gravity, a power greater than those collisions, yet gentle enough to shepherd even the smallest dust and gas particles into place. This was a time suitable for planets to form, and a time for one planet, the earth, to sustain life forms taking energy and substance from the planet without destructive impacts. It was the time for self-propagating plants and animals.

It was a time for making the surface of the planet suitable for another life form —a time for God to create the crowning glory of all his Creation, humankind. This was a time when all of that Creation acquired an even greater image of the Creator than before: cosmicwide physical beauty and order peaked into human consciousness made even more in the image of the Creator. This was a time for humankind to begin consciously responding to the Creator, spirit-to-spirit, heart-to-heart—something the Creator had intended since time immemorial.

In contrast to previous seemingly endless time, humankind grows in intellectual acumen by leaps and bounds. It is a time when intelligent human fabrication is possible. It is also a time for human choices; and willful choices begot the time when deliberately chosen evil invaded this paradise. Yet, the virtue to choose Godlike good blossoms in the soiled paradise garden even amidst the allure of evil. And so, it is a time for future-changing choices—either to be responsible caretakers of a common good or destructive predators.

There was a time when a wise and reflective citizen of the Old Testament Hebrew nation, was inspired to record his reflection on how humankind had been, sometimes wisely but oftentimes not so wisely, dealing with life's demanding and history-forming challenges. Thus he somewhat poetically wrote:

> There is an appointed time for everything,
> A time for everything under the heavens.
> A time to be born, and a time to die;
> A time to plant, and a time to uproot the plant.
> A time to kill, and a time to heal.
> A time to tear down, and a time to build.
> A time to weep, and a time to laugh.

5

A time to mourn and a time to dance.
A time to scatter stones, and a time to gather them;
A time to embrace, and a time to be far from embraces.
A time to seek, and a time to lose;
A time to keep and a time to cast away.
A time to rend, and a time to sew;
A time to be silent, and a time to speak.
A time to love, and a time to hate;
A time of war and a time of peace.
(Eccl 3, 1-11)

It is a time for sometimes small steps and sometimes giant leaps toward the common good of all. It is a time for Creation's many originally endowed gifts to further develop and enrich the earth. It is a time for hunting and gathering; for cultivating and manufacturing; for building and improving; for developing cultures. It is a time for establishing nations, kingdoms, and empires. It is a time for emigrations and the intermingling of cultures and accomplishments. But as the author of Ecclesiastes implies, it is not a smooth process without many pitfalls into evil and suffering. It is a time for much banging together and breaking asunder within humankind.

In the fullness of that time, a human Star, Jesus of Nazareth, brighter than any of the earlier explosions of stars and galaxies, a Star long awaited by humankind, a Star destined to outlast any of the stars of the universe, a Star that would not bruise even a frail reed in a swamp, that fullness of time when this bright Star would walk upon the earth and eventually bless it with a new life. He would neither bang nor break anything or anyone. He would be a simple carpenter's son claiming no burdensome allegiance, yet drawing all people to himself. In him all Creation would find its healing salvation, its peace. His name would be Emmanuel, God with us. Creation had reached its high point and was now possible to be even more at one with the Creator in the person of this long-awaited Star. The life and teachings of this Son of Man and Son of God would have lasting and determinative effects on the course of humankind.

In an awesome moment of that time, at the end of his life on this earth, from a Cross to which he had been banged, and seemingly incapacitated in a tomb, he gloriously rose to a new life that infinitely exceeded Creation's first inception. It was a time for humankind's crowning glory. All Creation was blessed by this new Star announced by a simple point of light in the night sky shining from a faraway star—a point of light that may well have begun its cosmic wide journey toward the earth at Creation's first beginnings. It was a time for previous Creation to usher in a new Creation. Thus ends the short narrative of Creation's beginning and culminating in the arrival of the One sent to heal the wounds of evil inflicted by the wayward ways of humankind.

In the following chapter, we re-enter the above condensed narrative of the earliest days of humankind and proceed in more detail through that history up to our own time. The narrative will not be detailed history nor will it pay detailed attention to human failings and correctives. However, we will scrutinize ourselves in the ongoing process of Creation, especially how the human family adapted to life on the earth. We will give special attention to how humankind responded to the self-revelation of the Creator; and developed ways of responding to the Creator, and how the Providence of the Creator provided for the well-being of humankind through the very processes of the evolving universe.

3

Humankind Enters the Creation Stage

Before the arrival of sidewalks and paved parking lots, streets and highways; before the advent of carpeted and tiled floors; before humans began living far from the ground in structures ever higher and higher; before we found ways of insulating ourselves from the natural surrounding air and environment; before we acquired what seems to be an aversion to the raw environment; prehistoric humankind spent a very significant and enriching amount of time on the bare ground among the natural materials of the earth. That open-air kind of existence allowed for a more undiluted view and experience of the earth and its environs that led to an amazingly practical-oriented wisdom. Pre-historic humankind had to develop practical ways of living on the face of the earth even without advanced scientific knowledge.

The regular reappearance of the night scene of stars and planets and comets and showers of falling stars prompted much speculation about what it meant. Even without the more exact scientific knowledge we are familiar with today, theirs was a very intuitive and receptive presence to it. Day in and day out, night after night, all the changing seasons, storms and earthquakes, winds, floods, upheavals of all kinds, furthered a special kind of knowing that literally shaped human life on this earth. This is so because the human physical and Spiritual makeup is designed by the Creator to learn from and be stimulated by Creation in all its manifestations.

Let us imagine families and clans are gathered around an open-air fire perhaps, and someone spots a falling star that may prompt a pause in activity. That event is commented on in quiet reverential tones. Stories and memories are recalled. Each one, young and old, feels something stirring in the core of their being. The entire family and clan grow with some kind of energy affecting and guiding them, influencing their whole lives. Activities are planned around the seasonal, monthly, and daily changes of these heavenly bodies. Winter cold, storms, and natural disasters are endured because the people are sustained by the energy of Creation itself all around them. Wisdom to know and respond to the experiences accumulates. Religious rites and rituals are developed to celebrate these events of nature and the God of it all. All this helped them through even the worst of nature's catastrophes and distresses. Through it all, the Creator is continuing the work of bringing Creation along a path to fullness.

We can only try as best we can to fathom the depth and breadth of their mythical science of the skies; but we must be cognizant of the fact that there was a deep wisdom in their intuitions that is beyond what we moderns can begin to understand any more. There was a psychology, a philosophy, a theology and a science of the universe all tied together for the sake of the grand epic journey of humankind down through earth and cosmic history. But even more than that, the very energy of Creation itself is pulsing through their being. The same energy that brought the universe into being is infusing humankind with the energy to keep pace with ongoing Creation, the same energy that pulses within the souls of humankind in our own time and circumstances.

More or less contemporary with those ancients were another people we call the Old Testament people who had their own mythology, their own way of expressing a similar understanding of the universe. The O.T. people based their lives on the earth and cosmos even without the knowledge of our contemporary science. Theirs was a very experiential knowledge based more on faith and inspiration.

For a few examples of where these images come from, read Psalm 19, 1-6; Psalm 29, Psalm 33, 6-9; Psalm 114; Sirach 43, 15-29; Sirach 40, 12-26; and many other O.T. citations could be found.

The Hebrew people reaped a rich harvest of wisdom and insight from their particular cosmos-based mythology. They encountered and reacted to their Creator God through this mythology; and the inspiration for their Religious Covenant Rites and Sacrifices was found in that same cultural Aramaic closeness to nature and cosmos. Those who have studied that culture and language say their very language reflects this earth and cosmos connection; and accordingly, the prescriptions of the Torah were Creation centered. (Cf. the Book of Exodus and especially Leviticus.)

And so it does not seem to be a mark of ignorance that the New Testament author, Matthew in his Gospel records a story of three Wise Men from the East following a star to find a person arriving on the scene of human history

(Mt 2, 1-6). If we today can only escape from our straight linear thinking, we too might come to appreciate that the stars in their own incomparable way would know that the Messiah was to appear. If, as science tells us today, the stars remember the 'big bang' of Creation, so too the birth of the Messiah, an even more momentous event than Creation's physical beginning, could be broadcast somehow to intuitive mystic minded scholars. However, this is not science, this is faith, and faith has its own surety, the surety of Divine Inspiration.

In these our own times, we have our own contacts with that same star-studded environment. Our visual contacts have been augmented with many truly marvelous technological advancements. No one before our time ever had the view of the universe that we have today through our telescopes. Surely, there are few people who are unaware of the photographic wonders available to us in so many venues. However, our sciences, unlike those earlier cultures we have taken notice of, do not and cannot speak of the Creator because the spiritual realm is beyond physical science. While our best science cannot envision a spiritual Creator, the Creator has imbued our sciences with the ability to know the universe in ever-greater detail thereby enriching our first source of knowing the Creator.

Those earlier people were not blocked from knowledge of the Creator as are our scientists because their purpose was exclusively to find the Creator and to respond to that Sovereign of the universe. The Creator revealed himself and imbued those searchers with a profound faith, though they were not without their own inexcusable faults leading to wars and appalling injustices. Without doubt, we today would be better off if we were interested in more than facts. The facts we know seem to cloud over our understanding of the more important matter of what it all means and where we are going with our expertise.

The photograph of the earth taken as our astronauts journeyed to and from the moon, is probably the most influential view of the earth anyone has ever had. That photo has been reproduced over and over again, so I am sure few have not seen that blue sphere of the earth showing the swirling clouds above the vast oceans and land masses suspended in the blackness of space. We will never be able to think or feel the same way about the earth or the far reaches of space. In that photograph earth seems alive, beautiful, and yet fragile. It actually looks like a livable place. People of letters and learning literally rhapsodized about a newfound sense of the earth, a recognized paradigm shift in human imaginings and thinking.

As Archibald Macleish wrote on Dec. 25, 1968, after the return of the moon travelers, "To see the earth as it truly is, small and blue and beautiful in that eternal silence where it floats, is to see ourselves as riders on the earth together, brothers on that bright loveliness in the eternal cold—brothers who know now they are truly brothers." A new impetus is given to the way we humans think about ourselves as inhabitants of this earth.

Maybe now a sense of responsibility for this earth will have a chance to catch up with our technical knowledge, which some perceptive observers of human history speak of as having inflicted a kind of wound to the soul of modern Western people. It is likely we are never going to be healed of this wound until we regain a Spirituality, a sense of our spiritual selves. Perhaps such a Spirituality can grow from recognizing the earth as home.

Home has always provided the secure place where life can thrive; but our concept of home must expand to include not only the earth but all the universe. A Spirituality based on the concept of home as a small plot and building one can call one's own will not serve us today. Our enhanced view of the earth and universe has given us a unique opportunity to develop a new concept of home and a Spirituality to suit that expanded concept. The concept of God we can now develop will be even more extraordinary than the God of the Biblical people. Only a God of cosmic proportions will be able to claim our allegiance and give us the effective guidance we need. Consequently, contrary to the Old Testament sense of it, we cannot claim a promised land less than the universe itself.

Actually, even the non-Hebrew ancients did know a God of cosmic proportions, and only such a God could have drawn them along the path of development they had to traverse. They knew and worshiped sometimes several Gods reigning from on high among the stars, who, if they were careful to not displease them, gave them their courage and strength in the daunting perils of nature. It might be a safe bet that they could not have endured their perilous conditions without faith in an abiding deity. Anthropological studies suggest an almost universal belief in a God of some sort.

However, earliest humankind had to enlarge their notions of God so their prayer and worship could enhance their lives more. Their notion of a fearful god who scared them into unhealthy and unwholesome ways had to become the God of Abraham, Isaac, and Jacob, of Moses, and finally the Father of Jesus. That progression was an astounding growth in faith stimulated by constant openness to the inspiration of the Creator known to a great extent through Creation.

We need give serious thought to the possibility that the gruesome practices of those earlier cultures were really not too many steps below the callous and sometimes horrid results of our contemporary cultural and scientific enterprises. We may well be as thoughtless and unaware of the consequences of what we are doing as some of those earlier people were. We still do industrial things in the name of our supposedly advanced technologies that have devastating effects on the surrounding populous, effects that may include the physical, psychological, or economic effects.

It may be that our contemporary concept of God is too small and misguided for us also today. Our notion of the Creator/God must continue to progress under the inspiration of Jesus of Nazareth, otherwise we may not hear the call of God, but may continue to hear only the siren call of our own works, and continue to suffer the consequences of our excesses.

First, as human inhabitants of this earth, then as Christians, we have very serious crises to work our way through today. It is becoming obvious to many that our technologies must be redirected so they enhance rather than destroy life on the earth. As Christians, we need to assimilate more fully the Gospel message of Jesus. The earth was so rich for him that his best stories centered on earthly matters.

Never did he preach "love the earth," but his appreciation of it was so profound we do well to pay attention to that. We may be missing something very important in his command of universal love if we fail to discern the full breadth of that love he intends. To avoid harm to ourselves and others certainly includes doing no harm to the earth we live on. Whatever we do to the earth we do to one another. This is an obvious amplification of his law of universal love.

Our source of wisdom will be the same source from whom the ancients as well as the Old Testament people and the Gospel people learned, the Creator himself. However, it is not enough to acknowledge God as Creator. We need to sense the heart of the Creator. The Creator was not just all head—making things. Everything God made God loved and cherished. Given all we know from Divine Revelation, it would seem God also loves and cherishes the good and beneficial things of which we are capable. Our best accomplishments will always be life-giving, as was the Creator. And anything that jeopardizes human advancement along the journey of Creation can only be evil.

Our technologies are God-given, and we do well to make the most of them. It seems to be part of the Creator's plan that we contribute to the well-being not only of ourselves but also of our earth—yes, even of the cosmos. We are responsible for what we do to the earth and what we may eventually do to the universe. Michelangelo expressed it well on the ceiling of the Sistine Chapel where he painted the hand of the Creator reaching out toward the hand of Adam to impart life—an awesome image.

The Creator reached out to Adam and imparted life. When we reach out to the earth, it is within our Divine-like prerogative that we too impart life. That, in fact, is why we were created in the image of the Creator—not just to play around on the face of the earth, but to contribute to life on the earth. What an awesome privilege! And what a shame to ignore our genuine calling. This applies not only to industrialists but to each and every human being born on the face of the earth. It must begin with the one who tends a houseplant or mows a lawn, or just walks along a path. If it does not begin there, it will never transfer up to the more prodigious enterprises that mark our contemporary times.

4

A Creation-Centered Spirituality for Earth-Living

Sparks, though small compared to the fire from which they are spewed forth, are impressive in their own right because of their eye-catching subtlety and beauty. They also possess the capacity to create more fire. The human spirit is a small spark made in the image of the Divine Spirit. This spark of the Divine Spirit within us is profusely responsive to all the physical elements that make up our earth, even our entire universe. This spirit-spark of ours can respond in joyful excitement to the eye-catching sight of a simple yellow dandelion springing up from between the cracks of a sidewalk in early spring, as well as the copious beauty of the summer season with its countless sensual experiences of the earth coming fully alive, and then can revel in the myriads of autumn colors that cover a landscape, and the winter snow that covers everything in a white blanket, all signifying the ongoing seasonal changes that are part of the richness of this earth.

In responding to all these stimuli, our spirit comes to know its Creator. In addition, attentive persons will discern humankind is the caretaker of this earth, because just as whatever the Creator brings into being is sustained with enduring, loving providence, so too a proportional providence is obligatory for humankind made in the image of the Creator. The spark of our spirit resonates with the sustaining fire of the Creator, spirit to spirit; and a human Spirituality emerges vitalizing ourselves as stewards of Creation.

Actually, it is natural for us to develop a Spirituality that is Creator-centered; but unfortunately, it is also possible to become excessively science-centered and create a very material-centered spirituality. Earth-centeredness is not the same as material-centeredness. A material-centered Spirituality will be self-serving and not Creator-serving because material possessions all too easily

14

become the focal point of our lives. Possessions may well be God-given gifts, but without a solid grounding and appreciation of their place in Creation they lose their Creation value and take on our own self-serving valuations. The physical sciences that have contributed to the manmade composition of so many things we possess become more compelling in our estimation than their original place in Creation. We become artificial-minded verses Creation-minded.

Our sciences and industrial enterprises are easily corrupted by unworthy and even dangerous ambitions. They are not a sure means to a lasting future *on their own*. Science is a marvelous acquired gift, yet without the enrichment of a faith Spirituality, it cannot promote the future for which we were created. Our ultimate purpose is a closer union with the Creator, and ungraced science and economic endeavors can never by themselves further that goal. Acting contrary to our original design does not make for a fulfilling individual life or culture. In fact, we have unwittingly inflicted a wound on ourselves and the earth, a wound that needs healing.

But this wound is never going to be healed until we regain *a Spirituality of earth living*. Such a Spirituality can grow from recognizing the earth as home. Home has always provided the secure place where life can thrive; but a concept of home as a small plot and building one can call one's own will not serve for this Spirituality.

We have made the entire earth our dwelling by utilizing earth-wide accumulations of the physical components we deem essential for the life we expect. We have made ourselves dependent on the artifacts of our industries which depend on utilizing the elements of the earth gathered from far and wide. It is not just a plot of land and a house that provides our needed security, but enormous portions of the earth's surface. In a real sense, we *occupy* the earth; but the question is, do we call the earth *home?* It would seem not so.

Yet our familiarity with the universe and the place of the earth within this universe makes it possible for us to form such a universewide home-Spirituality. As our spirits reach out and respond to an ever-expanding awareness of Creation, our sense of the Creator will grow proportionally as will our Spirituality. The Creator himself is leading us to this new Spirituality of earth-home. It is part of our Creation-mindedness intended by the Creator. We were created to be at home on the earth.

While ancient human cultures had little or no science of the realm of the sky, the God whom they knew and whom they worshiped slowly but surely led them to develop ever more advantageous ways of living with one another and with the earth. How to live benignly on this earth and with one another will always be an essential effect of any Spirituality. Those ancients, over the span

15

of many generations were able to improve their lives according to enlightened notions of God. A faulty sense of the nature of God makes it difficult for cultures to develop more just and benign ways of living together. If God is perceived as self-occupied and focused on his own glory, devotees of such a God will be the same.

The Biblical story of Creation found in Genesis is a story stemming from a people who were only interested in *who* did it—a Divine Creator did it; and the time it took was of no concern to those folks. The imaginative details of the six-day Creation process possibly helped promote in the minds of those people the concept of an awe-inspiring Creator. However, parts of that Biblical story have led some to serious misinterpretations of the rights and privileges of humankind over the earth.

One example is the tendency of advanced cultures to extreme exploitation of the earths' resources for the sake of possessions may have grown out of the notion that the Creator intended humankind to dominate all other creatures and resources of the earth, based on a misguided literal interpretation of this line from Genesis 1, 28: "Have dominion over the fish of the sea and...all living things that move on the earth." This may even have led some to the notion that we progressive cultures are superior to people of lesser, backward cultures who are satisfied with less material possessions. But if the possession of a superabundance of material wealth is perceived as a sign of a progressive people, this may well be the sickness of our culture that has led to a pervasive materialism.

Contrary to this, through a Spirituality that is derived from close spiritual communion with the Creator known from Creation and from Sacred Scripture, humankind is capable of acquiring a corrective to our current style of life, especially our resource-exhausting materialism. We may well have failed so far to develop our spiritual potential, having been distracted by lesser goals and potentials, but the fullness of our being is still intact. We have been created "a little less than angels" says the Psalmist (Ps 8, 5-8 titled *The Majesty of God and the Dignity of Man*).

A creation-centered spirituality is possible for us and would be much more beneficial than our material-centered attitude. Witness how so many are frantically searching for 'fulfillment' in excessive possessions and yet sadly do not know fullness of life. When Jesus said he came that we might have life to the fullest, it was obvious he did not mean full of possessions.

The parable of the birds of the air and the flowers of the field who possess full life bird and plant style thanks to the Creator, lays out what he meant by full life. Full life comes from sharing Creation's bounty with those around us like the birds of the air and the plants of the fields do. They neither plant nor spin, yet Creation supplies their needs. That is the Creator-designed economy for plants and birds and animals.

We do plant and spin yet still do not seem to be able to satisfy our insatiable longing for a more satisfying life. A Creation based spirituality would possibly produce an economy assuring sufficiency for everyone because the earth was designed to supply adequate necessities for everyone without the need for accumulation of vast resources. Without a guiding Spirituality the common good gets little attention. Without a guiding Spirituality economies become biased toward those who already possess the means for accumulating more, and the imbalance between the haves and the have-nots is destined to increase. Without a Spirituality many will come to believe their abundance is a God-given right, and the plight of the have-nots is just the way it was intended to be.

The Word of God that brought all things into being is still speaking to us through that Creation as it has all down created history, and that Word also speaks to us through the Words of Jesus the Christ spoken from among the suffering inhabitants of the earth to whom he has been sent to bring healing Salvation. It is a Word that does not return to the Heavens until it has accomplished the end for which it was sent (Isaiah 55, 10-11). That Word is as fruitful as seeds planted on the earth, and Jesus trusted that just as the Creator made the earth sufficiently fertile for life, so we have been created capable of even fuller life.

Now there is a spirituality suited for earth living that can be gained by viewing the Heavens in faith as we have been designed to do, and listening to the Words of Jesus of Nazareth that were totally in tune with the earth (Mt 13, 18-23). We are invited to consider what type soil we are and what might be obstacles within our soil that keep us back from more fruitful harvests. A fruitful Spirituality produces a more fruitful life on this earth.

5

The Universe Is the Soil that Grows All Life Forms; the Earth Provide a Garden

Soil, dirt, dust, mud, earth, are all the same thing and are capable of sustaining just about any life form you can think of, including our own human life. Science tells us the entire universe with its myriads of objects and colossal chemical reactions involving entire stars and even galaxies, over eons of time has contributed to the formation of this earthen soil and the accompanying life forms. So that means the entire universe is in a real way the soil that grows all material life forms. There is so much out there that we know very little about and probably will never see that has worked together for the common good of the universe and especially the good of the earth.

A physicist, Thomas A. Cahill, wrote in the August/September 2011 issue of America magazine: "[S]ince 1985 physicists have come to realize that the laws of physics strongly support the hypothesis that life itself is the reason for the universe, that it is not just an accidental smear on this rocky planet." Evidence is accruing that suggests the entire universe, as scattered as it is over space that cannot even be measured, began from a minute, compact bit of matter that has constantly been evolving and expanding through a process of interactions among its many atoms and particles and eventually interactions among stars and galaxies, continuing on down to this time. Science cannot detect or name a Creator of all this, but faith leads believers to know a Divine Creator of that whole process.

Just as it takes the precise amount of a lot of components to make a tasteful loaf of bread, so it took many different cosmic components to create our delectable earth. Any good soil needs the right complement of a lot of different minerals and chemicals so it can produce food for all the different life forms that depend on it. Then there are the elements of moisture most beneficial in the form of rainwater, and equally required sunshine in just the right proportion.

Science explains precisely how all these chemical intricacies naturally evolved over millions and even billions of years through a very random process. From the point of view of faith, we can surmise that it took a very *humble* Creator to allow the time required for all that to happen *in total freedom* (cf. John Haught's *Evolution and God's Humility*: "The nature of Divine love…logically requires that God would leave room in nature for randomness or accident. Love by its very nature cannot compel, and an infinite love should not be expected to over-whelm the world with coercively directive 'power'… Indeed, we should not be surprised that an infinite love would in some sense restrain itself, precisely in order to give the world 'space' and 'time' in which to become something distinct from the creative love that made it.…It is a humble love."

The intent of the Creator seems to have been that all those myriads of galaxies with their billions upon billions of suns and stars and accompanying bits and pieces of not fully formed matter exist out there as a form of Divine Providence especially for the common good of human life. How incredibly thoughtless it would be for people of Faith to be indifferent to that growing realization of science. The Creator made this world just for us and some kind of proportional faith response is obligatory from human inhabitants of this earth.

It seems probable that the more we give attentive consideration to the cosmic wide valuations of life intended by the Creator, the less we might be prone to all the life-destroying ways of which we have been guilty—endlessly repeated wars that achieve very little of lasting good for humankind; deadly punishments for crimes that also accomplish little toward rehabilitating individual and communal life; indiscriminate abortions all too often chosen for slight reasons with little thought given to the long-term effects on the individual or society; so many life-threatening byproducts of industry; all done in the name of some imagined 'fuller' life. The Creator made this earth and its environs just for us, so some kind of proportional faith response is obligatory from human inhabitants of this earth. While death is inevitable for any life form, whether human or animal, plant, insect or amoeba, humankind has not been given the freedom by the Creator to determine when human life will end.

Human life exists in communities of mutual dependencies for the sake of enhancing security from evil and fullness of life for everyone; and accordingly no one's life is going to be full unless all have equal rights to life. Human life is too precious to be sacrificed to any other value. Everything on this earth has some inherent life value, whether human, plant, insect or stone which must be respected—-not all equal but creational value none the less. The physical cosmos itself shares in this value because it came from the hands of the ever living Creator.

Humankind is awash in so much life on this earth and has such astounding capabilities of contributing to the ongoing amplification of every life form including our own, that we are obligated to think always in life terms. It seems a logical assumption that because the Creator himself is so vigorously and wholeheartedly alive, anything he created could not help but share in that life in some way. Until we can begin reflecting in that vein, all our rationalizations to decide who or what is going to be allowed to live will be deadly to all life.

No matter how one looks at it, the universe is a prodigious, majestic, and awe-inspiring work of ingenuity, praiseworthy and magnificent. While Creation certainly does redound to the honor and glory of the Creator, the Creator's own free purpose was to bestow a share of that glory on Creation. Every great and small bit of it bears the imprint of that glory and magnificence, and humankind bears a very special facsimile of that image in the faculties of intelligence and the capacity to make choices. Consequently, the wise dictum from antiquity often repeated: *The glory of God is the human person fully alive.*

Our earth, though an almost invisible speck of matter amidst such inconceivable quantities of stuff out in the cosmos, is marvelously entwined with the universe. While this universe has powerful effects on the earth, we who live on this earth also have the potential not only to affect the earth but more and more to insert ourselves out into cosmic space. Out there our capabilities for good will be greatly amplified, but we will also be capable of continuing to plant the seeds of malfunction and evil. Hopefully, if we do venture out to plow the soil of the universe, we will have grown to sufficient maturity through much wiser stewardship of the earth that we will have the fortitude to resist our typical inclinations toward dominance and self-centered advancement. Therein resides one of our greatest assets, our capability to learn and grow. That too is fullness of life.

4

The Cosmos Unconsciously Remembers Its Creator; Humankind Conciously Responds

So many ordinary, everyday contrivances have memories these days, and not just computers. Any digital appliance, clocks, coffee makers, phone, cameras, and cook stoves have a memory chip. No sooner were we settled in with these things, when astrophysicists discovered that the basic particles that make up all physical matter have a memory of sorts. To be precise, these scientists say it was the tremendous jolt of coming into existence that left an indelible mark on those particles that they call a memory. It is a memory that does not fade nor get jarred awry. Natural Creation never forgets its inception.

When the Creator planted humankind in this garden planet earth, the universe was well on its journey of expansion and evolution; but now it continued its journey under the gaze of human understanding as well as Divine. Now conscious spirit touches conscious spirit—God and Creation are bonded in an ever deeper and more marvelous manner. We have little or no records of the precise words or rites of earliest humankind indicating how they responded to the Creator, but plenty of evidence shows that they did recognize a Creator, and so since earliest human times then Creation has consciously responded to the Creator.

Of course we have ample examples of how the Hebrew people in Biblical days worshiped and prayed. Their religious Covenant life originated on Mount Sinai as they began their long wilderness journey to freedom from the Pharaoh of Egypt (Ex 12, 37-41). It was on that mountain where Moses experienced overpowering physical displays of nature that prepared him to hear the Creator announce the Divine intention to establish a Covenant with the Hebrew people. During his time in prayer after that experience, the Creator inspired in Moses the details of a Covenant between the nation and their Creator. Those awesome forces of nature exercised potent influences on Moses and eventually on the religious Covenant life of the Hebrews. It gave Moses the energy he would need to lead this irresolute people on their long journey to a promised new land and beneficial future.

Years later, while they were settling into that Promised Land, the poet King David was inspired to compose many songs of praise and worship called Psalms. These songs arose partly from their closeness to the Creator experienced in their natural surroundings, but most especially were inspired by their Covenant practices and prayers. We have a treasure trove of Psalms and other writings in the Old Testament attesting to the Hebrews' Creation-centered culture and religious Covenant.

Many Prophets and other holy Spiritual leaders of the people helped develop a profound Spirituality keeping them in close contact with the guiding influence of Yahweh. Even though they were oftentimes vacillating in their faithfulness to the Covenant, their faith response to the Creator left them and future generations profound and enriching literature and Sacred Rites to inspire many generations to follow. That covenant and the corresponding Spirituality growing out of it have been foundational for the Church in the Christian era.

The high point of all Creation and human life came when Jesus of Nazareth began to traverse the earth in his life's journey among this Covenanted people. Creation is now blessed with one who will respond to the Creator in a way no one before him had ever been able to respond—as the only begotten Son of the Father. This was the fullness of time all Creation had been waiting for during long eons of time. Now the earth and the universe have a voice fully adequate for communion with the Creator. This voice is also fully human, representative of all humankind, and in fact, representative of all Creation.

It is also the peak moment in the Religious and Covenant journey of the Hebrew people leading to a new and everlasting Covenant in the blood of Jesus the Messiah. This Son of Mary and (supposedly) Joseph died on a Cross that had been planted like a tree in the earth on Mount Calvary. New life enriching the universe would spring up out of the physical matter of that horrible site, the site of life-giving death. Creation and a New Covenant people are conjoined in a new and marvelous way even greater than the Old Covenant people had been bonded with Yahweh. Creation and humankind now join in a more gifted universewide response to the Creator. "Behold, I am making all things new!" (See Revelation: the entire chapter 21 and especially 21:5.)

All of this Covenantal prayer and practice profoundly enriched the life of Jesus of Nazareth. Jesus was resolutely and devoutly faithful to the Law of the Covenant, a Law he said would never pass away, though through him it was tending to fulfillment in a New Covenant. We can be sure he prayed as any devout Jew prayed, which would have included public and community prayers in the Synagogue and Temple. Much of this prayer practice included recitation, or more likely, the singing of the Psalms. His love for the earth and all things growing upon the earth might well have prompted him to sing out robustly and wholeheartedly the Psalms and other songs that were part of Synagogue and Temple practices. It is not likely Jesus was a passive participant. Given whom he was, that voice not only rang out around the synagogue, but also rang throughout all Creation.

In these our own times, it is within the Church that the combined voices of Creation, old and New Covenant voices, and the Word of God spoken by Jesus of Nazareth, have been resounding. That combined chorus is a spirited voice reverberating all throughout the universe. Unfortunately, in these later times, the voice of Creation has become subdued and hardly accredited within the Church, even though the Old Testament Psalms with their creational grounding are constants in Liturgy.

It is deplorable that Creation gets limited attention in spite of the fact that in these times we have greatly improved ways of observing the earth and the universe through our scientific technologies. Our attention is on physical phenomenon that can be observed and studied for science purpose, while faith and Creation get relegated to an obscure place. Pope Benedict XVI, even while Cardinal Ratzinger, repeatedly decried this situation (cf. *In the Beginning: A Catholic Understanding of the Story of Creation and the Fall*, Wm. B. Eerdmans Publishing Co., Grand Rapids, Mich., 1995).

Physical science of course cannot know the Creator because it only knows what can be physically experienced. Yet the *faith science* that has developed through millennia of Spiritual contact with the Creator can still lead us to the Creator. The darkness of unknowing that afflicts physical science can be enlightened by this faith experience of a personal relationship with that First Cause of all things. This relationship of faith has produced in our own days profound poetic, musical, and artistic responses to the Creator. Some of the most profound poetic expressions are the prayer expressions between persons of faith and the Creator. Words of prayer have been enlivened to soar to new heights of veneration and worship. Faith, hope, and love are given spirited impetus in the hearts of many, yet Creation languishes in Ecclesial expressions.

One nineteenth-century poet of faith, Gerard Manley Hopkins (born 1844), in awe-filled poetic expression wrote, "The world is charged with the

23

grandeur of God," and in another poem, "We cannot touch—even name God with us—apart from our experience of a world that is charged with the grandeur of God. Every moment of every day fleshes the Divine presence. God touches us in the same way that the world...touches us—calling, inviting us to become more human. If we answer with all that we are—and hope to be—then to live is to live in the faith that we have found, that we are at one with an incarnate God. The meadow is not God—you are not God—the patterned morning freshness is not God. But to open yourself to meadow and morning, to what is before you, is to find Emmanuel, to know God-with-us as life in the moment."

It is unfortunate that many of us are held captive by insipid minds that fail to appreciate fully the natural cosmic manifestation of the Creator. Conscious response to the Creator is often tepid and low-keyed and not really productive of faith growth. Prayer responses are kept from soaring to the heights of expression that could be natural responses to the fullness of the Divine known from contacts with Creation. We are kept down to levels of expressions that our minds reason out for us; and so poetry like that of Gerard Manley Hopkins above does not fill us or flow from us. In some sense, we cannot be fully human without exercising our full capacity as persons in communion with the Creator.

All humankind, including the Church, suffers some kind of diminishment when faith responses to the Creator diminish. Cultures, social values, individual initiative, arts, and sciences suffer. Contrary-wise, conscious, affective, and intelligent response to the Creator can enrich all aspects of human life; we are made that way. Creation cries out to respond to the Creator through our human responses. It seems evident Jesus intended his Church to be a contact with Creation from which can come that fuller life he so often spoke of, but our detachment from Creation within the Church stifles that purpose. Furthermore, our role as stewards of this earth garden has suffered terribly.

7

A Twofold View of Creation as Viewed from the Visible Universe and from the Viewpoint of Faith

The same natural earth and universe that academic science views and studies is viewed by people of faith and is named Creation. That is so because through the self-revelation of the Creator faith detects the signature of the Creator stamped on everything. To perceive this Creation stamp does not need science, but those sciences do serve to enhance the faith appreciation of the Creator. We have not even begun to know the physical extent of the universe with all its varying dimensions and vast areas beyond our ability to see; and the glory and light of the realm of the Creator will always be beyond what either faith or senses can detect. Yet we are designed for and are invited to inquire into the abundance and richness of all that, whereby we also enrich the sense of our own identity and fullness of being.

One of the most valuable assets of Creation is its potential to lead us to the Creator. We will never be able to comprehend fully the Created universe without an accompanying sense of the Creator. To know the Creator we need a source of knowledge that is beyond the scope of our sciences, and that source of knowing is the Divine self-revelation that we gain from observation of the universe. Faith knowledge and natural human knowledge complement one another, and we really cannot fully exercise the one without the other especially when it comes to the universe. Both the physical universe and the Revelation we gain from observing that universe are the most comprehensive fundamentals of our human life, the most exhilarating and life-giving experiences of which we are capable. Moreover, all this was available to us even before the use of any artificial aids because the Creator designed us that way.

The Word of Creation spoken from the realm of incomparable light and magnificence imprints everything brought into being with an endowment of that grandeur of the Heavenly Realm, be it the smallest bit of matter that can be known only by the most advanced technologies, or the colossal, far away planetary objects that can only be seen by the use of our most advanced telescopes. Each detail of that Creation fills out in some limited way the image of the Creator. *Creation is not an extension of the Creator*, that is, not part of the Creator as some heretics have mistakenly believed, but is the readable handwriting that the Creator provides for us to read.

Humankind has been on a faith and science quest for a long time, yet the Creator does not scorn our imperfect images of the Divine. What is required of humankind is to strive to improve our concepts of the Divine so we do not create faulty images in our minds' eyes that lead to practices that do harm to one another and to the earth we inhabit. Without doubt, we today need to follow the example of earlier humankind who were able to grow in their concepts of the Divine and reexamine our own concepts of the Divine. We still seem to bedevil our lives with what is unhealthy and even destructive, going contrary to the intent of the Creator we seem to have misinterpreted.

We are very distinctive Divine image-bearers, and easily equate what we know and can do, even what is not good or healthy, with the will and purposes of the Creator. A more reflective attention to the universe around us can provide a corrective to those faulty notions. Because we have grown physically and spiritually from the soil of the universe, the basic integrity and goodness of the universe is innate in us. We need only open the doors and windows of our being to the vitality of Creation and the Creator will renew and enliven us with the very energy of Creation itself. These are not things we can make happen by anything we know, but they are potentials inherent in our very being. It may be that we have built up barriers to nature and the universe by insulating ourselves within so much artificiality. Nevertheless, Creation still beckons us even in the materials of our manufactured contrivances.

The Old Testament people, culturally conditioned to live in close proximity to nature and the cosmos, were constantly exposed to the Divine Revelation inherent in their physical surroundings. The Creator God was the center of their lives and worship. Because of their unique receptivity to the God of their Covenant, and under the guidance of Moses and many holy Prophets, they grew in a unique closeness to Yahweh. Their sense of the Creator was profound and is inspirational for us even today.

These people have bequeathed to us a collection of sacred songs called Psalms, mentioned in previous pages, which were inspired to a great extent by Creation. Any song worth singing, so good singers can tell us, has to have been truly inspired. Otherwise, it is not going to inspire the singer to give a great performance, nor will the listening audience be inspired. Great songs have inspired great deeds in individuals and in nations all down through history. In fact, all artistic inspirations carry overtones of the Divine. Outdoor nature and any of the components of Creation have always been a rich source of Divine inspiration.

Creation is full and rich in the ingredients that make up our human lives, and contemplation of any of its many facets stirs mind and emotions. The song, the singer, and the audience can all be caught up in the vibrancy of the universe and of human life that is such a vital part of that universe. Consequently, through these inspired Old Testament Psalms and other writings, we are able to experience a people stirred by the grandeur and magnificence of Creation, not only to worship and celebrate the Creator, but also to shape their lives in concordance with Creation. So much of what the Old Covenant Law prescribed for the Hebrew people was actually beneficial for them, and was suggested by the beneficence of Creation. In other words, they recognized and cooperated with Divine Providence provided through Creation.

Efforts on our part today to augment nature by mechanical contrivances can be beneficial too as long as we do not go contrary to the overall tendencies of Creation. Creation tends to evolve and diversify, and human beings gifted with the potential to utilize nature's elements and processes, actually contribute to that on-going process. The Creator did not deem it necessary to create all the synthetic, manufactured items we find useful and enjoyable because we were given the capability to do just that. Because the universe has been designed to enhance all life forms, earthly nature tends in that life-enhancing direction. An ingenious Creator made it all work together that way.

No matter what lens we use to look at the earth or the universe, whether it be the lens of our sciences or the lens of faith and Biblical inspiration, and no matter how we name it—universe or Creation—we are looking at the soil out of which we acquired our being. In fact, even our spirits have grown from our earthly and cosmic associations. We are planted securely in this soil, and it is extremely fertile soil. Our potentials are as vast as the universe. We do well to stand in awe of our natural potentials, yet we cannot expect infinitude for either this universe or ourselves. We are limited, but we need not let our limits hold us back from even aspiring to an undreamed of future.

8

The Star-Building Potential of Creation
Is an Actual Grace for Humankind

There are certain English words that are exquisitely meaningful and even pleasing to read and pronounce. Two such words are *grace* and *graceful*. Grace is a word and concept that can be elaborated on with abundant synonyms: beauty, elegance, refinement, kindness, benevolence, dignity and so much more. Individuals gifted with personal grace enrich others by their presence and often can even moderate discordant behavior. The concept of *gracefulness* possibly derives its special significance from the way it reflects a special attribute of Divinity itself, namely, God's graciousness in so many providential ways.

Even during the earliest phases of Creation, the Creator had humankind in mind. How could he not, given that this living being would be created in his own image? Everything else created would be designed for the good of humankind. Divine Revelation tells us this is so, and even contemporary scientists are reasonably sure the universe is designed to give sustenance to all life forms, especially human life. Secular science probably calls that the laws of physical matter; believers in a Divine Creator call it Divine Providence.

The special design of the earth is a gift of Divine Providence; and to use a term of our Catholic theology of Grace, it is an Actual Grace, or Divine gift, intended especially for the good of humankind. That Grace has enriched the earth and human life infinitely more than any human trait of gracefulness. We know that many particular Actual Graces are showered upon us through persons, nature, and events, but we have paid little attention to the tremendous Graces bestowed on us through the agency of the universe. The earth and the universe, including all the billions upon billions of stars and galaxies "out there" are all bearers of that Grace of Divine Providence.

What the beauty and grandeur of the earthen landscape bestows on our lives is recognized as a marvelous Grace; but we have yet to appreciate the proportional effect of the landscape of the universe and its extensive Grace. Nevertheless, our minds and hearts were created to comprehend and to gain from the many-faceted, life-enriching benefits of the universe. When we recognize and take to heart this Grace of the universe, our whole being is enriched; it is the way of God's Graces. We can open our minds and hearts to this cosmic offering the same as we do when we view the lesser beauties of earthen landscapes, or we can pass it by. That inattention dries up our spirits that naturally thirst for the stimulation stemming from the source of our physical being.

Because we are Divine image-bearers, the Creator's Providence enriches our natural faculties of mind and will in some limited way with the very creating energy that brought the universe into existence. This is exemplified when creative persons produce great works of art or when inventive industrialists and technocrats ply their trades to the benefits of humankind. Many of these talented persons acknowledge special stimuli stemming from different sources, sometimes it is gifted family backgrounds, education, opportunities, any of which can be called Actual Graces. Moreover, some even admit to direct Divine inspiration. This is all God's gift to humankind.

At this crucial time in social and cultural development, humankind needs extraordinary resources of energy or Grace for a future that will require even greater creativity, ingenuity, and especially the development of ethical and moral values favorable to the good of the earth and human society. Just as nature's forces of earthquakes, volcanoes, and other massive erosion processes are constantly building the surface of the earth, so too do all the varied human works of building and fabricating add something to the surface of the earth— either for good or for harm; and more importantly, add to the building of human culture and community.

This earthwide enterprise also requires energy for correcting and healing the wounds caused by past misguided, self-interested enterprises. The wounds of humankind and the wounds of the earth will not be easily healed because they have been festering for a long time. Too much rapacious greed, too many starving and sick people left unaided, too much malicious deception about the causes of injustice and inequality, too many wars, too many weak and ill-conceived attempts at resolutions of local and international disorders, and too much disappointment and despair.

A common flawed belief seems to be that Creation is something the Creator did long ago in which we have no part. The attitude seems to be, it is the

Creator's work, we dare not, cannot get too involved. Consequently, we look around at the universe and assume we have nothing to do with it, and the universe has nothing to do with us. Most of it is out of sight and seemingly out of touch. It seems to be just a vast array of real estate and resources for possible exploitation. Certainly those resources were created for our benefit, but we are privileged to have greater involvement than that. Creation is very complex and multi-faceted, and so are we.

The truth is, earth's inhabitants have so much more to be gained from the universe than economic gain; and that universe has much to be gained from us. Because we are co-creators and stewards of the earth, once we go further out into the universe, we will be obligated to extend our earthly responsibilities to where ever we go. The Creator obviously had a plan in mind that implicates humankind and the universe in mutual ongoing benefits; but we have not begun to look into the full implications of that interdependency. To ignore the impact humankind has upon the earth and will inevitably have upon the universe at large is irresponsible; and to ignore the many benefits the universe provides for our well-being is to ignore God's Providence.

Professionals in the field of science as well as most lay folks today marvel more and more at the wonders of the universe we are learning about through contemporary sciences. Yet religious teaching and leadership remains mostly silent about the Spiritual advantages to be gained from experiencing that universe. Every physical frontier humankind has ever traversed has expanded the human spirit to ever-greater creativity. Our next frontier will quite likely be the far reaches of the universe. It is in the nature of humankind to be restless, a trait planted in us by the Creator himself.

More often than not though, reference to Creation by many in Christian Churches is limited to the Genesis story of Creation in the Bible. Of course, the Genesis story is an authoritative resource for knowing the Divine source of Creation; but contrary to some interpretations, that story gives very limited factual details about its coming into existence because the story was not intended for that purpose. It was a faith-inspired story that opened an avenue for earlier humankind to the Grace of Creation that led them to develop their human capabilities, and to live in harmony with the earth and with one another. That story was and is still is beneficial for Christians today. While we may rightly ignore the science deficient assertion that Creation was a six-day process, we dare not ignore the wisdom to be found in Genesis, and its value in understanding our relationship to the earth and to the Creator.

Earliest humankind had little science of the earth or of the sky above to guide them, and consequently could not express themselves in our contemporary scientific terms, whereas our lives today are centered on science and technologies. For us today who are very much into keeping time and into matters scientific, that Biblical Creation story lacks the powerful dynamism and awesome energy of the evolutionary processes that contemporary science describes. In this age dominated by science and technologies, our faith concept of deity must be comparably stimulating and inspirational. Scientific evolution theories provide just that stimulation. Fortunately, the Grace of Providence also resides in the multitude of sciences. The Creator has led us to these sciences and will not contradict our efforts.

The intellectual tasks to understand what will be required for a very different future, and the will to do what is right and just, will require the Graces of Creation itself. Human enterprises are becoming immersed in ever more complex processes, requiring ever more difficult judgments about the common good, and the moral rectitude to do what is right. It will require more than good science and virtuous intentions. Yet, God's Graces always build upon and strengthens those human capabilities and intentions, which by themselves are often inadequate. As a contemporary poet has said, "Affairs are cosmicwide now!" And cosmicwide graces are required.

In the earliest moments of cosmic evolution, the basic material particles that make up the material of our earth and our own physical bodies went through unimaginably complicated physical processes far out in space. Our contemporary science tells us it began with minute basic particles of matter that coalesced into ever-larger masses of material that eventually become stars and our own earth, and finally galaxies. It is an awesome science that studies and describes all this, but while this chapter is based on that science, it will not be concerned with scientific details for their own sake. In other words, this will be a reflection on the scientific description of the creation processes.

Accordingly, consider this extremely condensed biological explication of how our physical bodies acquired their material substance during the gestation period in the womb of our mothers who were nourished from the food that grows from the earth that is made up of material compacted together long ago far out in space. Then after birth we continued to grow physically from the same conglomerated food we ourselves eat.

That process of our physical "body building," while not nearly so awesomely stupendous, is in its own way as marvelous as the cosmic processes of the formation of new stars that grow from the material of exploding Super Nova stars. A new structure grows from acquiring (eating) from the menu of that scattered cosmic matter. Many might be familiar with all of this from contemporary TV science shows.

Because our physical roots reach all the way back to that star building process, the Grace of Divine providence for evolving humankind is comparably vigorous and dynamic. Because our physical roots are in that cosmic star building process, the Grace of Divine Providence for evolving humankind is comparably vigorous and dynamic.

As a nonscientific, literary aside, on a clear night, gaze up at the star-filled sky and experience the sensation of dizzying sensitivity to the view. Assuming the contemporary science alluded to above is correct, every physical particle in our bodies once existed "out there"; and consequently, we may be experiencing a real life equivalent to what is described in the movie *E.T.: The Extra-Terrestrial*, in which E.T. longingly states, "E.T. [wants to] go home!" On a more serious note, because we come to know the Creator from our experiences of the universe around us, it seems entirely likely that the Creator is beckoning to us from this experience to go out there and come to know the Creator.

Concluding these minute details, we now jump ahead to present day human realities, and consider some features of our contemporary situation. Our present circumstances are not as simple and restricted as in earliest days of human history. We are no longer hunting and gathering to provide food, but are utilizing earth's resources in much more exploitive and too often despoiling ways, often to the detriment of our own well-being as well as that of the earth.

To rein in the insatiable demands on these resources and our detrimental use of them will require more than better science. It will require wisdom and insight to discern values and goals we have not been accustomed to taking into consideration. We must be able to foresee a future very different from what we usually think about. Left on our unaided recourses, we will be prone to build the same short-sighted social, economic, and political structures that bedevil us today.

There is always high hope for the future of the earth and of humankind, but unfortunately for too long we have been driven by lesser goals and expectations. We have yet to give thought to the hard to believe Graces of Creation, though anything less will not serve our advancement to the future that awaits us. That future is cosmic wide and kingdom deep, meaning the Kingdom Jesus always spoke about.

There has never been a moment in the course of human history when extreme crises and discord between nations and cultures have not strained human capabilities beyond their limits. Despite this, who of us does not marvel how individuals and entire communities can recover from devastations of a tornado, a flood, a tsunami, or how entire nations can recover from all the accumulated effects of war, especially the effects of two world wars. These are events that try the souls of the best of individuals and nations, situations that can lead to despair, yet often make individuals and communities even stronger. It is nothing less than the Grace of Creation that explains such possibilities. The Creator has made it so.

It is easy to foresee that the future may possibly contain even greater dangers or harm. Our potential for harmful deeds gets stronger even as our potential for good results gets better. We have miles to go in our journey on this earth and within Creation, yet the human person created in the image of the Creator is suited for the journey. We think too small if we do not envision greater possibilities for humankind than what we have usually thought possible. Nonetheless, we remain vulnerable to extreme crises beyond our capabilities if we do not recognize and open ourselves to the Grace of Creation. We cannot build stars or galaxies but the awesome energy or Grace that went into their evolving existence is available to us as Divine providence suited to our situation. There is a built-in 'app' for just that—-the Grace of Creation.

We need look beyond the multitudes of technological marvels that have contributed to a life style never before known on the face of the earth. There is progress in all that to the benefit of humankind, yet we are called to nothing less than an entirely new way we approach our enterprises on this earth, and not just new technologies or better ways to do things. We are called to a Creator-based care of the earth that will lead more surely to the common good the Creator intended. It is a common good that leads to the fullness of Creation. That calls for thinking big and expecting much.

9

A Call to a Creator-Grounded Care of the Earth

Most of us are very aware of the growing number of homeless people. These statistics reach into the hundreds of thousands. Even without a personal experience of being homeless, the sight and thought of this situation make us feel uneasy because home is so crucial that we do not even like to think about being homeless. Unfortunately there is more than one form of homelessness, both scary and possible.

It is unfortunate that few if any of us can actually think of losing our earth home. That seems unthinkable and even impossible. We have forgotten that recent generations experienced many years of what came to be called the Cold War, and the defense strategy of mutually assured destruction (MAD). It was a time when our earth home actually could have been destroyed, yet the possibility of actual earth homelessness has failed to remain imprinted in our minds.

Nor has it sunk in that we are trashing our earth on a massive scale that is destroying our home in another way. For some reason, the many devastating conditions affecting the earth do not ring sufficiently loud warning bells. The matters that grab our attention are national and international security and economic crises, which are pertinent concerns, but need to be considered in the much wider context of earthwide economies and security.

All too seldom is the welfare of the planet earth included in local and international deliberations and actions taken. Efforts to curb destructive industrial processes and to clean up subsequent toxic waste are not planned and executed on the scale necessary to keep up. The goals and procedures are too limited because they do not take into consideration that earth and human needs cannot be sustained without reference to their earth/Creation grounding. Fortunately it is slowly dawning on many that our well-being depends

34

on the vitality of the earth. The many deep wounds inflicted on the earth must be attended to before we can hope to find health and healing for humankind.

In order to acquire the right perspective on matters that will help us in these most difficult times, we need an appreciation that care of the earth is really a *sacred* matter of Creation proportions. The earth and its inhabitants are sacred because they come from the "hands" of the Creator, and exist in fond attention within the heart of its Maker. The universe is not just a transitory interest, but has the eternal and constant attention of the Creator. The universe is God's sacred Creation, and humankind is the special beloved of the Creator.

We traverse the earth for a very lofty purpose. The story of Creation and especially the Creation of humankind found in the book of Genesis speaks of so much more than a Creation process. The Genesis story speaks of a relationship between the Creator and the earth, and an even more remarkable relationship between the earth and humankind. We do not just populate the earth, but we have a sacred relationship to it. Relationships establish very special connections of respect, appreciation, esteem, and love. Consequently, we are mistaken if we view the earth simply as an inanimate object to be used and built upon. Inanimate though it may be, humankind is *matter of its matter*, in an analogous way that Adam acclaimed Eve, built up from his own body, was *flesh of his flesh, bone of his bone*. Humankind and the earth share a bond of extraordinary relationship established by the Creator himself. For that reason, the universe is not just a collection of scattered stuff, and humankind is not just an accidental part of it. It exists in a relationship of mutual needs and support.

Because the majority of humankind seems to feel no special relationship with the earth as home, some have acquired an attitude that leaves us free to traverse recklessly over the face of the earth assuming absolute dominion over every other created thing. We feel free to take what we want and never mind the consequences to the earth. It is after all, only an impersonal "it."

Because what we know about our Creator to a great extent comes from what we observe of our physical surroundings, to destroy the earth is to destroy the source of our faith; and to efface the earth is to efface the image of the Creator stamped on everything. We were created to be builders, growers, developers, life givers; but when we become destroyers, that goes contrary to who we deep down know we are. We were created and ably equipped to be caretakers of this vibrant part of the universe; and functioning as responsible care takers of the earth is the only way we can live up to this God given identity and reach our full potential.

Earth and cosmos have breadth and depth that broaden the mind, the imagination, the emotions, and our very souls. Earth and cosmos are so much physically bigger than we are that we cannot get our minds around it all, yet our very souls pulsate with the energy inherent in its make-up. Too many lesser manufactured things are called "basic" to our lives for which many aim, but small basics lead to inadequate efforts. There is nothing more basic to our wellbeing than recognizing Creation in everything in and around us. Creation is God's work, and the Creator declared it good.

Bumper stickers come in a mixture of varying value and worth, sometimes expressing humorous triviality, and sometimes more disreputable contents of the human mind and imaginations, and occasionally they soar to lofty contents of inspired wisdom and truth. One such timeless burst of human insight says it like it really is: "God does not make junk!"

10

In Other Words, Call It Ministry to the Earth

Ministry is usually thought of as a service. Many governments have official Ministries serving the needs of various segments of the population according to the dictates of laws and constitutions. Church ministry is always considered to be Biblical directed, intended to lead members to the common good of all according to the intent of the Creator as expressed in both the Old and the New Testaments. That is precisely what our life on this earth could be, ministry leading to the welfare of the earth and of humankind. That way our lives become Christ and Creation-centered, Biblical-directed.

The Biblical story of Creation found in the Book of Genesis reveals what the people of the story had come to understand about their relationship to the earth and their relationship to the Creator (Gen 1, 1-31). They understood that the Creator had honored them by giving them everything in the garden as gifts. Their charge was to tend to that garden (Gen 1, 27-31). Humankind is honored by the gift, and needs to reciprocate with responsible use. Giving names to everything (Gen 2, 19-20) implies finding use for it all. There is practical wisdom expressed in that story that can lead to advantageous use of the gifts of the garden. The storytellers also understood that Adam and Eve (humankind) had abused their gift of the fruit of the garden. Almost for sure they understood that the imagery of the Genesis story was symbolic. Their stories always were mainly mythical in order to teach values.

Unfortunately, our inattention to that Biblical wisdom has resulted in our continued irresponsible way of living amid the gifts of the earth. These gifts were intended to bring about something more than marvelous intellectual achievements and amazing technologies. That too, but the Creator had a vision for even greater ongoing creative activity in which we share. Great technologies are not capable on their own of leading humankind to develop fully our spiritual potentials. Great technologies do not produce their greatest good if they are not guided by enlightened objectives—Creation objectives. Furthermore, possession of excessive amounts of material goods provided by the Creator easily degenerates into a materialism that leaves the spiritual area of ourselves lying dormant. Then we are not leading full human lives.

However, the more we become mindful of our lives as ministry to the world, the more we will acquire a new mindset that does not aim at domination and exploitation, but rather cooperation with earth's ongoing processes. This will actually lead to even greater accomplishments augmented by Creation's natural giftedness. Too much of our effort has gone against Creation's natural tendencies. We may have to let go of what we think are everlasting certainties—that endless exploitation of natural resources will always lead to better life; a better life always requires something artificial; the natural without artificial enhancements is dangerous or unsatisfying. Surely, our contemporary experiences of so many disappointing results of what we are doing should leave no doubt that most of these so-called certainties are misleading and are not at all certain.

We literally think too small when we think only in our usual economic, scientific mindset. There is an earth economy based on cosmic economy that always tends toward the common good of Creation. Genuine beneficial human economy is based on such earth and cosmic economies. Ministry to the earth will always put us in line with the Creator's own objectives for Creation, and then we are sure to utilize our own gifts to their best advantage. The Creator has great things in store for the human enterprise, and we do our best when we think in Creation proportions.

The story of the Tower of Babel in the Book of Genesis (11, 1-9) epitomizes our contemporary situation in a remarkable way. The builders of the tower were actually *too restricted* in their vision. That tower was actually too small to fit into the Creator's plan for humanity. They were wasting materiel and probably genuine superior building techniques to satisfy very limited and limiting goals of selfish glory. No wonder, as Genesis says, their social structures and ability to communicate broke down. Any time we try to go contrary to the natural tendency of Creation, there is a human price to be paid. Just as the builders of the Tower of Babel should have done, so we too have to think outside the box of our usual achievements. To think outside that box means not just higher and bigger, but outside that box—thinking Creationwide.

When we go that route, we will actually be less restricted because we will be following the mind of the Creator who is not limited by our short view of possibilities. The Creator's work is still not finished and we have the privilege to join in bringing that plan to fruition, and that plan is beyond what we can even imagine. If what we fabricate is genuinely in line with Creation, we may not always achieve something grand in the minds of all beholders, but there will be a deep-down sense of a good thing accomplished. It would seem that much of what humankind accomplishes genuinely gives that sense of a good thing accomplished; but it is important to be able to sense when what seems to be a great accomplishment may in fact be counterproductive for a more genuine good. That greater good can only be recognized in the broader context of Creation itself.

Yet we need beware of not making the same mistake Adam and Eve made in the Garden of Eden, thinking we can be equal to the Creator *knowing all good and evil*. The Genesis storytellers wisely recognized the folly of that mistake; they knew they had paid the price of losing their garden paradise. They let a good gift (exemplified as fruit from a tree in the midst of the garden) entice them to irresponsible actions. What started out as a life-fulfilling ministry of stewards of that garden became a devastating affliction, *working by the sweat of the brow* in an inhospitable environment, a condition of their own making. They traded a Creator-based ministry to the earth for an ill-fated alternative that brought them much grief. Paradise lost.

11

Our Stewardship of Creation in Union with the Risen Lord

Some scientists say they have evidence that new things might still be coming into existence far out in the universe. For physical scientists that means the universe is still evolving. For folks of faith, we also know that the Creator is bringing Creation to a new height in the person of Jesus of Nazareth who is sometimes referred to as a new Creation. In him, through him, and with him are the seeds of hope for the future, even though he was not a scientist. He knew the heart of the Creator and the higher possibilities the Creator had in mind for humankind.

Death, that is inevitable for all human life, did not keep him from Resurrection to new life. He rose to new life that now enlivens every other human being who is born into this world. Saint Paul, who had a unique experience of the risen Lord, writes about this life of the Christ and about our lives in union with him. We begin reflecting on two Scripture passages from the letters of Saint Paul in which he reflects on his experience and what it implies for others in faith and what it implies for all Creation.

First, from his Epistle to the Colossians (1, 14-19): "For it is in Christ that the complete being of the Godhead dwells, embodied, and in him you have been brought to completion. Every power and authority in the universe is subject to him. In him everything in heaven and on earth was created...for in him the complete being of God, by God's own choice, came to dwell." Again, to the Ephesians (1, 8-11): "In Christ he chose us before the world was founded... He has made known to us his hidden purpose...namely that the universe, all in heaven and on earth might be brought into unity in Christ."

In other words, in his own person, Jesus carries forward all of Creation to a common goal of unity with the Creator; and not only all of humankind, but everything on earth and in the heavens—stars, galaxies—all that stuff "out there" and around us. Of course, neither Saint Paul nor Jesus would have been thinking of galaxies or of anything we now know about the cosmos. They did not need the details we know today because the earth and universe they experienced in their daily lives affected their lives more profoundly without a scientific explanation than it does us today. Earth and universe were not just casual experiences for those people, but were very determinative elements of their lives. Therefore, these references of Saint Paul to "the universe, all in heaven and on earth" were not just poetic, verbal images. Paul was speaking of the real world as he knew it.

Probably for most of us today, such ways of speaking may seem naive and unscientific to be taken seriously. We know so much more about the universe than those Biblical people did. What they say seems to us to be just ill-informed talk, so we do not know how to take it. Yet, what Saint Paul knew of the universe was so much more transforming of mind and heart than all our technologically advanced knowledge is for us today. For Saint Paul, faith in the Resurrection of Jesus really centers ourselves right there in the center of all things. Saint Paul knew Jesus *is* the center of it all. Science can never detect that, but faith provides a surety greater than anything science can ever say about it.

By faith, we today stand with Christ in a profound Spiritual unity with the universe. All this gives special meaning to our citizenship on this earth and in the universe at large. On the natural plane, our lives are tied to the well-being of the earth and of the universe; but on the Spiritual plane, our lives now in union with the risen Lord bring us and the earth that fullness of life Jesus promised. This is Creation fullness, a fullness we have hindered by sinfulness.

Unity with the risen Lord places us also in unity with the *healing* love of the Redeemer. Not only human life, but also the earth, has suffered many wounds inflicted by our selfish utilization of its many gifts. Nevertheless, we really do have the capability to bestow healing to what we have thoughtlessly abused. With healing can come greater beauty and even greater utility. On the natural level, a well-tended garden, field, or landscape, by our hands actually contributes to the well-being of the earth. Now, on the spiritual level, through our lives in union with the risen Lord, we can be bearers of the special healing love of the Creator himself. Again, this is Creation-based actuality, a reality to which we have seldom been lead to give much thought.

As ministers to the earth in union with the risen Lord, even our efforts in physical ministry are enriched. Because of the serious nature of our earthly problems, some may look for miraculous intervention of Jesus or the Creator; but miracles are not needed. Our natural born gifts of mind and will are empowered by our unity with the risen Lord of all Creation. This is the foundation for hope that our human efforts to change our ways can bear fruit. This is the fullness of life Jesus came to bring us. This is Resurrection life in which we also share.

We are one with him as he is one with the Father. Those are not empty words. Those words are full of the new life Jesus now lives in us. Through us now, all of physical Creation is enriched and enlivened. This is our full ministry to Creation. Everywhere we plant our feet on the earth, everywhere we ply a trade of any kind, Creation is blessed and enriched. This is an enlargement of every kind of ministry we do for one another and to the earth. This is Resurrection stewardship. If we remain mindful of this full reality, we will not desecrate the earth or any little bit of it. If we remain mindful of this dignity, how can we continue our thoughtless ways? Jesus did not rise to New Life just for his own glory. He rose so we and all Creation can continue in glory.

But if our ministry is to bear fruit, the Christian community needs to celebrate in faith our spiritual bonding with the earth. For this end, when we gather to celebrate the Eucharist or any Sacrament, we need to develop an earthly awareness. We must not spiritualize the words of St. Paul or the words of Jesus himself as simple ideals. We celebrate the actual reality of our unity with all Creation through our unity with the Lord of Creation. From this unambiguous celebration of earth reality can come a deeper appreciation of our special place in Creation, which in turn can lead to practical deeds.

Because of the serious nature of our earthly problems, some may look for miraculous interventions, but the miracles are not needed. Our natural born gifts of mind and will are empowered for healing by our unity with the risen Lord. Humankind working in conjunction with the natural gifts of nature can bring about genuine healing even to the earth.

12

The Kingdom of the Beautitudes:
Pardigm Changes for Humankind and the Earth

For Christians today, the Cross is the defining image we use to express our faith in Jesus the Messiah. But for Jesus of Nazareth himself, the Kingdom of God or the Kingdom of Heaven was the focal point of his Spirituality and teaching. That Kingdom was the subject of the prayer that has come down to us called the Lord's Prayer: *"Our Father Who art in heaven, hallowed be thy name, thy Kingdom come, thy will be done on the earth as in heaven...*for Thine is the Kingdom, the power and the glory forever." This must have been a typical kind of prayer that Jesus prayed with his disciples, praying for the coming of that Kingdom of Heaven, and was a topic of much of his teachings.

The Kingdom of God was the realm of the Creator and therefore was a Kingdom traversing all time and place. Many Middle Eastern people in the time of Jesus of Nazareth thought of the universe as the realm of the Creator. They envisioned the Creator dwelling as a Divine Sovereign above the dome or firmament of the heavens. One might say the Creator made his home and Kingdom in Creation. In their thinking then, the Creator is more intimate to the universe than we think of it. We usually assign a place to the Divine that is separate from the universe—Heaven.

Over the span of time that humans have inhabited the earth, many kingdoms have come, and many kingdoms have gone, but the Kingdom of Creation/universe endures through all Creation time. Of course historians do not usually consider the universe as a kingdom but it seems Jesus did. This is partly due to his cultural Aramaic background. That spiritual Kingdom was in stark contrast to most kingdoms at the time that were seldom benign or benevolent.

The despot whom the Romans had set up to keep the people of Palestine in obedience to Rome was King Herod—not a benign ruler by any standard.

In the experience of Jesus and the people of his time, kingdoms were all too often agencies of total control and subjugation. Civil society and actually many of the religious cultures of the time were the source of much suffering and injustice for people. Military style revolutionaries as well as religious visionaries were constantly attempting to bring about changes in overbearing power structures, but they almost always replaced one malevolence with another. Boundaries of kingdoms and dynasties were in constant flux leaving the earth and people often with little relief from their pain and suffering. Jesus taught that the enriching benefits of this kingdom of God were antidotes for the healing and uplifting for individuals and cultures.

In line with this, the Beatitudes of Jesus were more than words of encouragement; they were promises of empowerment to the full life the Creator had always intended. For those who heard those Beatitudes in the depths of their hearts, they imparted a healing vitality and the potential for profound personal and cultural enrichment. The Beatitudes did not demand some kind of extraordinary effort to achieve their benefits, but proclaimed the gracious providential blessings of the Kingdom of God. Conversion from sinful ways and freedom from devastating social and cultural injustices could then be possible. The Beatitudes were promises of full life. The problem for some of the contemporaries of Jesus as well as for us today is the difficulty taking the Beatitudes to heart as fully as Jesus himself did. He experienced and lived the bounty of Beatitudes. Those who listened to him probably sensed he was speaking from profound personal experiences because he taught with personal authority as no one else they had ever heard.

How Blessed Are the Poor in Spirit, the Reign of God Is Theirs

This first Beatitude does not imply that people are expected to become something they are not. They *are* the poor in spirit; it is their lot in life. Yet even this physical and cultural poverty was not a deficiency for life in the Kingdom of Heaven. Besides these political and economic disadvantages, at the time Jesus was teaching, the people were experiencing a lot of negativity about their standing before Yahweh brought on by the way the Scribes and Pharisees taught the Law or Torah. If one did not live up to all the little details of the Law as the Pharisees taught it, they were guilty of varying degrees of fault. The Beatitudes of Jesus on the other hand were intended to inspire hope for such a spiritually and physically downtrodden people.

Jesus would never have given them imperatives that only a few especially gifted individuals could ever hope to accomplish, as the Pharisees taught. The Beatitudes do not say, if you act in a correct way you will receive the gift; but rather, the gifts of the Reign of God are your Kingdom inheritance by right of Creation. Neither did the term *poor in spirit* imply that those folks must achieve a sense of ascetical diminishment about themselves. The Reign of God was theirs by right of the valuation of the Creator himself, no matter their physical or social circumstances. Their value was Creator given, a Kingdom inheritance.

Jesus spoke often about the Reign of God or Heaven in his parables; and the Beatitudes brought that Kingdom home to them in pragmatic ways. That Kingdom was more than a spiritual ideal. It was a spiritual reality available to them in their real life situations. Through the teachings of the Scribes and Pharisees they had lost their Covenant Spirituality that gave them a sure standing before Yahweh, and consequently had lost hope for themselves. Jesus intended to arouse in them that inspiring and life-giving Spirituality. He often said the Law would never pass away and was still their saving Covenant with Yahweh. The Reign of God was their Covenant right.

Blessed Are the Sorrowing;
They Shall Be Consoled

While Jesus certainly did what is sometimes called kitchen-table counseling in the course of his travels and teaching, his words and deeds brought about real results beyond counseling words. Nevertheless, this was not some kind of miraculous effect because he was the Son of God. He knew himself and others knew him to be the son of Joseph the carpenter (supposedly) and Mary his mother. His life's experiences were culturally Aramaic, and his Spirituality was shaped by his prayer life with the Father and his spirited religious experiences of the Covenant. He lived the Covenant as Moses had intended it, untarnished by the later additions of the Scribes and Pharisees.

It was not just by accident that he accentuated this particular Beatitude because grief and sorrow were literally constants in everyone's lives due not only to the usual personal grief and sorrow from death or sickness, but often enough from the political and social situations that prevailed. Life tended to be very stressful and tedious. Very few persons or circumstances in their lives gave them real or lasting consolation. Everything including even family could be snatched from them at a moment's notice, whether by sickness, death or the instigation of political and religious authorities. Consequently, most people probably believed in the inevitability of ill fate.

In his second Beatitude, Jesus was saying that the consolation they could expect was going to be something beyond the ordinary meaning of consolation. It was the consolation that their sufferings were not futile because even their sufferings had within them the potential for healing. While sin and pain were inevitable, so too was the consolation of new life. It would not take a powerful warrior leader to bring about this new life, nor any change in governing authority. Such changes usually led to more of the same. But the Divine power of the Creator that came to them through the Covenant could bring about real enlivening consolation.

The second Beatitude was surely the fruit of many experiences of grief in his own life and many interactions with others suffering grief. This may well have included the experience of his visit with Martha and Mary after the death of their brother Lazarus as recorded in the Gospel of John (11, 1-44). John emphatically shows that Jesus was grieving with them. When he spoke to them about Resurrection to new life after death, he was also reminding them of something he often taught, that the consolation of this new life was theirs even on this earth because the Kingdom of God is already within. One does not need to fight a battle or learn some esoteric truth to acquire it.

The promise of new life in the Kingdom of God was also intended for relief from future grief he recognized his disciples would eventually experience because of him (cf. all of chapter 24 of the Gospel of Matthew, the beginning of calamities, and specifically 9-10, "They will hand you over to torture and kill you. Indeed you will be hated by all nations on account of me"). Consequently blessed will they be who mourn and grieve even as deeply as the first Christians were made to suffer in the Roman arena for the sake of the Gospel of Jesus.

Furthermore, as is becoming evident today, grief and sorrow do not end there, but will eventually arise stemming from human activities that afflict not only the inhabitants of the earth but even the earth itself. The consolation of healing from these wounds is beyond the expertise of professional practitioners of healing. These wounds are cosmic and earthwide. The healing must be of Kingdom/Creation proportions; but first, humankind must recognize the wounds and grieve a grief of soul depth. Without that grief there will be no Beatitudinal consolation.

These Beatitudinal gifts have obviously resonated in suffering hearts all around the Church and the world because nothing less can account for how so many can suffer so much and remain strong in faith. This promised Divine consolation can be the healing Grace and energy needed if and when we today finally begin grieving the terrible harm done to neighbor and earth. If we cannot grieve because of it, we may never be converted to better ways. Jesus recognized and experienced this consolation of the Kingdom, making him the healer that he was, and promised that we would be doing even greater things in his name.

Blessed Are the Lowly;
They Shall Inherit the Land

There is some degree of probability that for many of us, the lowest item on the totem pole of earthly dignity would be the dust of the earth. Housekeepers work endlessly to get it out of the house, perhaps fearful of germs, or because it is unsightly, or its presence is socially unacceptable. Furthermore, it is the ingredient in messy mud. Something might be considered as worthless as dirt; and in former times, to lick the dust was probably the worst punishment one could give an enemy. One could go on vilifying paltry dirt and dust.

In contrast, the topsoil made up of this dirt and dust provides fertile fields where precious food can be grown. Such soil and fields are highly valued and cared for. Then there is the value of real estate where homes, buildings, and financially rich enterprises flourish. Dirt and real estate mean different things for different people, and Jesus often uses the differing imagery in his parables and teachings. However, in this Beatitude he takes his teaching in a new direction. He is speaking of the *land* in a much more spiritual way.

The land or the earth is the dwelling place and throne of the Divine Sovereign. This is the Spiritual realm of the Creator, the Beatitudinal *land* or Kingdom of God. This Kingdom encompasses the lowest elements of dirt and dust as well as the productive fields and the highest valued real estate. It also encompasses the human inhabitants of this land as well as all the other living creatures. This Kingdom is teeming with life and all that is good and bountiful, shining with beauty and grandeur, the site of the original condition of Creation.

It may be hard for us to get our minds in line with the way Jesus spoke about this Kingdom because he envisioned enrichment we cannot even think about. The promise is extraordinary *fullness of life*, the fullness of life Jesus said he had come to give (cf. John 10, 10). That fullness of life makes for much greater enrichment than the riches usually thought of as fulfilling the human needs for power and dignity. This is the realm within which even today we live and move and have our being. It is as real as physical landscapes or real estate or earthly kingdoms. Furthermore, it is not something that can only be experienced in some future time—after death. It is a present reality. It is Beatitudinal reality.

To catch that meaning of *full life*, give thought to when we might feel the most alive on this earth. Sometimes it will be when we are just walking or working on the surface of the earth; or when we feel the giftedness of the earth; when we sense the grandeur and wonder of the universe; when we are involved in creative beauty; when human activity is functioning in peace and tranquility; when all seems well on the earth; and especially when God or Jesus are experienced in some exceptional situation. Such a sense of earthly life can be exhilarating, though it will probably be only in fleeting moments because most of the time we are too preoccupied with attention to lesser realities. The Beatitudes are intended to get us in touch with this full life in an even deeper way.

The words of the Beatitudes that we have heard many times usually pass over our heads because we do not hear them as literally as Jesus quite likely intended them. Often for us moderns, the words of Jesus seem just too idealistic; yet surely we recognize that Jesus was a realist. His stories and Beatitudes are not naïve fairytales or unfounded fiction. They are more realistic, pragmatic, and effectual than we usually conjure up as ways to make our way through life's many troubling situations.

In order to be fully engaged with this second Beatitude, we need give thought to just who are the lowly. Those whom the listeners of Jesus as well as most of us today consider lowly are the very ones who are promised this land dignity. The parable of the guest without a wedding garment is relevant to this (Mt 22, 11-14): "The reign of God may be likened to a king who gave a wedding banquet for his son…When the king came in to meet the guests, however, he caught sight of a man not properly dressed for a wedding feast… the king then said to the attendants, 'Bind him hand and foot and throw him out into the night to wail and grind his teeth…'"

Perhaps the unfortunate person mentioned in that parable who was thrown out of the banquet hall because he lacked a wedding garment was the one well-dressed, well-groomed and mannered, possessing all the qualities of a cultured person who naturally assumed that his dress and manners would be acceptable. Perhaps he did not recognize that the required wedding garment was ordinary human dignity, dignity that he maybe did not value or perhaps had lost by degrading conduct.

According to the story, the banquet hall was belatedly filled with those brought in from the byroads, both the good and the bad. The obvious implication is they all had the prescribed wedding garment except the one. The "bad" obviously possessed the garment that allowed their entrance to the banquet hall in spite of their faults. The only one considered without a wedding garment was the one lacking the sense that his real dignity was not in clothing or social standing. All this gives a remarkable, paradoxical sense of that Kingdom with which we can be blessed. The story revalues in effect much of the negative personal attributes we might think can keep us from being gifted—admitted to the Kingdom of God, while stressing there are arrogant personal valuations that do keep us from the banquet hall. It is important that we keep those differences in mind, otherwise we become discouraged with ourselves or we become complacent with less than our best.

As a rule, when we today reflect on these Beatitudes, we tend to think in our usual constrained ways rather than expansively as Jesus intended. Without the aid of the wisdom of Jesus expressed in the Beatitudes we will be left with to our own less-empowering thoughts which often leave us floundering in ineffectual efforts.

Blessed Are They Who Hunger and Thirst for Holiness; They Shall Have Their Fill

This Spiritual hunger and thirst Jesus speaks of are more than ascetical virtues, and the holiness spoken of is more than a quality acquired by virtuous activity or conferred from an outside blessing. This holiness is part and parcel with our being because it is the holiness of Creation. Everything is naturally holy because it comes from the hands of the Creator. To hunger and thirst or fervently seek to discern this holiness is to seek and find the Creator. This hunger and thirst leads to fullness of life we desperately seek.

For many of us Catholics, something is holy if it has been blessed with holy water. We may be unmindful that the article and we ourselves are already holy. Oddly enough, before the article was blessed we might easily have thrown it away as meaningless. There is some limited benefit to valuing blessed religious articles and places to be sure, but there is a devastating disadvantage to not valuing the holiness of all Creation.

To begin evaluating the meaning of this Beatitude, we will now consider the very down-to-earth human drives of hunger and thirst. Hunger and thirst are essential drives of human nature because without those physical drives we would not seek to sustain our lives. What's more, without hunger and thirst we would never enjoy the social benefits of food and drink. There would be no celebratory meals and banquets, no picnics, no enjoyment of chocolate, baking, and candies. Life would physically and affectively dry up without hunger and thirst.

But Jesus is pointing out another hunger and thirst as powerful and compelling as the hunger for food and drink—hunger and thirst for the holiness of Creation; and that hunger and thirst is even more vital than our physical drives. We quite likely have to train ourselves to value this Creationwide holiness to which we pay no heed, but unless we grasp that astounding significance, the Beatitude will have very little practical effect on our lives. We will not sense that we are actually leaving a real hunger unfulfilled—-the hunger for creational fullness. Without hunger and thirst for the holiness of Creation we will not seek the good of Creation or its genuine blessings.

Lacking that sense of the holiness of the earth, many scientifically advanced cultures including our own have been destructive to the earth; and without that hunger and thirst we cannot transform these destructive cultural tendencies. The consequent harm done is quite likely greater than we can even discern because of our long-time attention to the need to seek a living through some kind of personal gain that overshadows every other value. If I have achieved satisfying financial and social gain, what more should I value? We become immune to the collateral damages done to our physical and social environment.

Blessed are we and the earth and all its life forms when we recognize the gift of real God-given holiness and blessing. In this we and even our earth will have our fill. This Beatitudinal blessing can be attained simply by recognizing and honoring the basic reality of the holiness of all Creation. *To have our fill* as promised by the Beatitude will bring about a change for the better in the course of our entire life's processes.

Blessed Are They Who Show Mercy; Mercy Shall Be Theirs

The human virtue of mercy is being called for here, but it is a virtue not appreciated by many. Genuine human mercy is a reflection of the Divine mercy shown to all Creation. Though there is unimaginable inequality between the Creator and the universe, Divine mercy is freely and generously exercised toward the cosmos and the earth evident in all forms of Divine Providence favoring earth and humankind. Perhaps it is because we find it difficult to attribute such unanticipated and unrecognized mercy to the Creator that we find it difficult to value human mercy. Perhaps mercy seems like weakness, whereas it is really a sign of Divine-like strength and character.

How fervently must Jesus have proclaimed blessed are they who show mercy, mercy shall be theirs. Those who show mercy are given the assurance that they will be gifted with a special vitality and strength they usually never associate with mercy—a typical Beatitudinal gift. In a world that suffers immeasurably because mercy is not valued, the strength and vitality of this gift of mercy can bring about a lot of unanticipated good. Mercy to homosexuals, to prisoners of many kinds, mercy to those condemned to death, mercy to enemies of all kinds will all bring about much more good than seeking a kind of justice that is really nothing more than harsh and cruel judgment seeking revenge.

Mercy is a moral virtue and responsibility, yet for Jesus this Beatitude was no simple moral imperative as we might take it. Morality involved, yes; but he is not suggesting that some extraordinary virtue is required to receive this extraordinary gift of mercy. The physical and spiritual gifts inherent in all Creation flow freely from the mercy of the Creator. These are Kingdom gifts we do not gain by anything we do, but they enliven our lives in innumerable, merciful ways. This Beatitude is intended to open us to that gifted reality of Creation mercy, Kingdom of God mercy.

It is quite likely we may find it hard to think of showing mercy to the earth. Nonetheless, due to our special God-like gifts, we have been established as stewards of this earth in order to contribute to its ongoing Creation process; and surely one of the qualities required of a steward is mercy—fashioned according to the mercy of the owner. Reciprocal mercy to the earth can provide the motivation to make the changes we need to make and thereby bring about the good of all humankind. There is a Creation-based relationship between the earth and ourselves calling for just such mercy.

Blessed Are the Single-Hearted, For They Shall See God

It is a very difficult thing to watch one's nation and religious culture disintegrate into ineffectual and futile existence. More than one kingdom or culture has come to such an inglorious end. The Hebrew nation and Covenant practice was in the throes of such decay in the Gospel days. The focus of so many Jews was divided among so many overwhelming objectives; to overthrow the Roman rule, trying to deal with so many religious factions maneuvering for influence over the people, especially the Scribes, the Pharisees, the Sadducees and others; outrageous injustices by the Temple authorities and the Romans; ill-conceived religious reforms instigating ridiculous grandstanding for attention especially by the Pharisees were all weakening the religious and cultural fabric of the nation.

The Old Testament Prophets as well as Jesus in his own time were intent on making the Jews aware that genuine righteousness was more than appearances. To see this condition present in business, religion and governance must have been painful to Jesus of Nazareth and would have occupied much of his prayer time with the Father.

Many of those conflicting pursuits, some good in themselves, needed a single-minded focus and corrective. The Hebrew people were losing their single-minded attention to their Covenant with Yahweh. Covenant practices were becoming nothing more than cultural routines that benefited them no more than any cultural asset can. The Covenant Law was no longer able to uplift and refine every other aspect of the culture including social and individual mores, as it functioned in earlier times.

Disreputable and self-interested enterprises to provide excessive paraphernalia in worship and prayer promoted the practice of buying and selling supposed necessities for ritual offerings and worship within the temple area. This was a practice Jesus so dramatically objected to one day by overturning the tables of these businesses and chasing out the sellers. His complaint was that the House of God had become unrecognizable for what it was intended to be (Mk 11, 15-17). Jesus knew full well those people would be right back doing the same things. He knew violent physical action against an unwanted activity would never bring about what he wanted. It is never the solution. Those money changers and merchants would only return with improved equipment that would barricade themselves from any further disruptions.

All of this could well have prompted this Beatitude: *Blessed are the single-hearted, for they shall see God.* The Beatitudes of Jesus provided Spiritual assets for personal renewal not because they contained detailed instructions in moral or religious matters. He was not saying that what he did was the way to deal with such things. Rather, in his Beatitudes, Jesus gave assurance that the way to the full life they wanted and deserved, free from evil, was within them, the gift of the Kingdom of God. This is no manmade construct. Jesus is proposing in his Beatitudes a way toward deep-down transformation in their attitudes toward life within their nation and Covenant worship. No mere human endeavor could bring about the changes in thinking and practice needed for in-depth renewal. Today it might be called a paradigm shift in how they viewed their relationships to nation and Covenant life.

A deep-down experience of the Divine has caused many a cultural paradigm shift. Moses experienced the Divine as probably no one before had ever experienced it, beginning at the top of Mount Sinai where he discerned Yahweh inspiring in him the Covenant amidst awesome natural displays. That experience had an astounding transformational effect on Moses and on the course of the history of the Hebrew Nation. Yet that same kind of experience is not necessary for everyone everywhere. Seeking such extraordinary experiences leads many astray from God because they are seeking personal satisfaction. But blessed are the single-hearted who seek only to see God and not their personal satisfaction through extraordinary experiences. The Beatitudes do not lead to such experiences but to simple transforming Divine providence coming from the kingdom of God that is within themselves.

Those who recognize the Creator in all the fascinating magnitudes of the universe especially as we know it today actually acquire an even greater sense of the Creator than Moses had. The gifts of the Kingdom of God and of Creation itself are gifts available within and do not need extensive searching outside oneself. It needs to be said here that this Kingdom of God is also experienced by many faithful souls in direct interior infusion of Grace during prayer and reflection. God is not limited to Creation when revealing himself. Yet even interior movements of the Spirit might well be instigated by prior experiences of the outside world.

It is easy for us in our time and culture to be similarly double-hearted because too many unconsciously take faith for granted. Too many unconsciously take faith for granted and accept most cultural values without really evaluating them in the light of faith. On some big hot-button social and religious issues many do take a stand, but too much of our culture is accepted unquestionably. Consequently faith and culture that should be complementary to one another are actually two separate and often contrary categories. We make ourselves double-hearted.

Blessed Too Are the Peacemakers; They Shall Be Called Sons and Daughters of God

There may be no other ingredient of human society more valued than peace, yet most endeavors to achieve it have been woefully unsuccessful. Peace is the stuff that has occupied countless hours, even years of national, tribal, and ethnic statesmen and leaders, and breaking of peace has broken the hearts and lives of countless individuals and nations. Peace is obviously more easily reflected on and talked about than put into effect. Poverty of ideas perhaps induced by low expectation of what humankind is capable, roadblock the path. It is not at all surprising that Jesus included the pursuit of peace in one of his Beatitudes.

One of the most ill-conceived ways to peace all too often encouraged by Religious leaders is to pray for the death or destruction of one's enemies. While it is always seen as a sign of faith to pray for peace, all too often little distinction is made about what we should pray for. Unfortunately this kind of prayer actually leads to moral decadence. The Old Law that "thou shall not kill" and the law of universal love that Jesus taught, namely to love even our enemies, are watered down and compromised; and any genuine foundation for judgments about what constitutes justice and moral good are corrupted. Consequently, it is assumed that peace can only come with the destruction of one's enemies. That path to peace has not been very promising in spite of so many white-knuckled prayers like that. Such prayer is the exact opposite of this Beatitude that leads to profound Creation peace.

The second half of this Beatitude: "Blessed too are the peacemakers, they shall be called sons and daughters of God"—actually gives the best hope for peace: *to discover we are sons and daughters of God*. To help appreciate that Beatitude, consider some reflections on the actual Creation-centered foundations for peace that constitute us as children of the Creator. The entire universe was created in silence and peace, including the earth and humankind, and consequently peace is actually innate to us. We possess that attribute of peace even before we begin using our minds and wills to plan for peace. Silent peace reigned during the creation process.

Contrary to what is probably the usual conception of the Creation process, it was begun in peace and proceeded in peace. It just *silently* came to be. It is probably only our propensity to be noisy and constantly working against obstacles that causes us to imagine Creation had to be noisy. The motion of everything speeding out in all directions after coming into being was a smooth, quiet process with nothing to hold it back, entirely free to follow its own unobstructed course. It was all beautiful; it was good; there was supreme peace; a peace wherein all things could become what they were created for. Moreover, the Creator declared it good. There were no ingredients of evil anywhere. There was certainly much banging together of objects small and gargantuan which would have caused noise in our atmosphere of air, but none of it was going contrary to the laws of natural matter causing a disruption of its natural peace.

Jesus calls peacemakers sons and daughters of God because just as sons and daughters are equipped with the genes of their parents, so too has the Creator enriched us with an important determinative trait of our being, those peace genes of Creation. Jesus, of course, knew nothing about genes and genetic sciences but he did not need to know all that. He was inspired by Old Testament writings and his heavenly Father to know that we are sons and daughters of God. That is surer than any science can teach. His Aramaic listeners did not need our science, but contemporary science provides these genetic details that fill out the picture for us today.

That peace mentioned above still reigns supreme throughout the universe except here on this tiny garden planet earth. The human inhabitants of this earth, patterned after the image of the Creator himself with freedom of choice, also have the capability to be instigators of *evil* that can destroy peace. Even though we have chosen noisy, damaging war time and again, the Creator has made humankind capable of being the stewards of all Creation including the peace of Creation. An awesome and seemingly impossible responsibility for such unpeaceable people—stewards of peace! All the same, overall, humankind has probably been in peace more than we have been at war, which seems to indicate we do have the capacity to be peaceable. After all, it is in our Creation genes.

To our disadvantage, we seem not to appreciate that as image bearers of the Creator, we really do share in some limited way in the very peaceful creative energy that brought all things into being. Unfortunately, our willful efforts to bring about peace in the midst of a very unruly world often remain ineffectual because our basic Creator-given potential for peace remains hidden and unrecognized deep within our being. We rely almost exclusively on the powerful yet inadequate gifts of mind and will, both of which have been weakened by the effects of evil; and we leave dormant the innate peace gene that is part and parcel with our created humanness.

Scientists refer to the "big bang" to describe the beginning of the process of the universe coming into existence, but actually it was a sudden surge that was not a noise bang. It all just silently came to be. We assume it had to be noisy like we always are, yet at the same time we do instinctively long for silence in the midst of so much noise in the world now. Actually, we do not need some kind of extraordinary faith or contemplative prayer to find that silence. The instinct for quiet and peace is in the very composition of our being, having been made from the dust of the earth that is naturally permeated with silence and peace. Before we can be willing and knowing makers of peace, we need recognize that the potential for peace already resides at the core of our physical being put there by the Word of the Creator. By this innate DNA we are sons and daughters of the peaceful Creator.

Besides this, Christians desiring to be peacemakers have access in faith to the very Word of the Creator, the Son of God. This is the One whom Saint John in the Prologue of his Gospel eulogized so eloquently, saying: "In the beginning was the Word, the Word was in God's presence, and the Word was God. He was present to God in the beginning. Through him all things came into being, and apart from him nothing came to be" (Jn 1, 1-3). This same Word is spoken through the Spirit of Jesus to all who long for peace. This Word is not an instruction to be followed or a peace plan for the nations of the world. Rather it is the empowering *Word of Creation* itself. The Creator needed only say the words "let there be light," and there was light. That very creative Word is spoken to us and consequently is implanted in our very being. Christians attuned in faith to this Word will discover, as obviously Jesus knew, that the silence and peace of the Creator is all around and within us. This awareness possibly prompted him to proclaim that we are *children of God*.

This peace even remains in the physical landscape that is disputed and fought over in wars. The very blood shed in violence and war can be productive of peace because that life's blood has also been imbued with the peace of Creation. As this blood mixes with the earth, the potential for peace becomes stronger. Witness the peaceful cemeteries of war fatalities. Walking the rows of the markers one can experience the mixture of the terrifying noise and brutality of battle and the peace that seems to rise out of the very soil. "If here, why not everywhere?" seems to be a mournful, plaintive cry coming from those peaceful graves. Our war heroes bequeath to us not only the valor of loyal service, but maybe even more importantly, the unspoken message that peace need not necessarily be contested for in this nonpeaceful way.

This peaceable earth under our feet and the Word of God spoken to listening hearts are constants that never lose their effectiveness even after contrary deeds and words. Mind and willpower are superlative spiritual gifts of our human selves capable of superlative achievements, yet to be successful in making peace, even they do well to refer humbly to this innate capacity for peace found in the very fabric of our physical being. From those combined Creator-given resources we are capable of making peace.

Additionally, all this has been augmented by the Resurrection potency of the risen Lord, when in the upper room after his Resurrection from death, Jesus conferred peace upon his gathered disciples. "Peace be with you, my peace I give you" (Lk 24, 36). They and we are a Resurrection-gifted people within whom peace now resides. That conferral of peace was a God-given gift through which the genes of peace that reside within us are enlivened. Peace is part and parcel of our new life in the Resurrected Lord.

The Beatitudes of Jesus speak about profound realities we undoubtedly cannot conceive of on our own. Jesus is speaking of that fullness of life he always promised. Full life presupposes peace, and in fact is impossible without peace. We need not be forever frustrated because of our inability to make peace because that kingdom already resides within us. That may seem like a fantasy to us, a pipedream, but the dreams of Jesus were not fantasies. They were inspired by his closeness to the Father, the Creator.

Blessed Are Those Persecuted for Holiness' Sake; the Reign of God Is Theirs

Jesus probably included persecution in his final Beatitude because he experienced it often himself. However, he no doubt also experienced himself gifted within the Reign of God that he spoke about so often. Jesus did not speak about abstractions but about his own real life experiences. He was speaking out of the experiences of a unique personality that might not have been appreciated. Even his parents sometimes had a hard time understanding where his uniqueness led him, as at the age of twelve when supposedly he was lost in the Temple. Many acquaintances may well have chided his parents for not reining in that son of theirs. And once he began his public ministry, many might have predicted that taking such a countercultural course that he prescribed would lead to a disastrous end for him and for them if they followed him. True uniqueness is seldom appreciated.

Predictably, remaining true to his principles did put him in serious conflict with the Temple authorities, a situation that actually led to plots on his life and eventual death. Yet his trust in the Father and the Reign of God gave him unfaltering courage and resolve. He instinctively knew that all this persecution and suffering was taking place within the Kingdom of God where the work of the Creator is coming to completion. These blessing are the Divine Providence of the Kingdom. The Beatitudes of Jesus were intended to put suffering humankind in touch with this Divine Providence of Creation.

Out of this faith and these experiences coalesced his Beatitude, "Blessed are those persecuted for the sake of holiness, theirs is the Kingdom of God." He knew the blessings of that Kingdom so here again he did not speak about abstractions but out of personal experiences. Jesus did not have very much "book learning" other than what he learned from Synagogue teachers, nor did he need all the details that took up so much time of the Scribes and Pharisees. He had enough simple human wisdom to see that that so-called learning did not help those Rabbis understand the Law, nor did it help others whom they were supposedly leading. That is why people would say he spoke like no other teacher; it was obvious Jesus knew whereof he was speaking.

To understand better the particular blessings and rewards of this Beatitude, we need reflect further on this Kingdom of Heaven that he says will be our inheritance. As a cultural Aramaic he had a sense of the connectedness between our life on this earth and our life within the vast universe. For those people, things belong to a much bigger picture than the eye sees or the mind fathoms. Such people will not see everything through lenses like ours that can only see straight-line logical processes. For them there are many facets of life that can only be accepted as awe-inspiring mystery.

Jesus gave them a highly enhanced meaning to their cultural mysteries and values. That meant there was more to life than even their culture and Covenant Law ever spoke about. It could not have been his explicit intention, but he was actually preparing his disciples for the new Covenant he would establish in his blood on the Cross. His Beatitudes were more than instructions for the here and now, but were laying the groundwork for the fulfillment of his teachings.

Jesus did not have a concept of heaven as totally separate from our earthly existence as we do. Resurrection from the dead, yes; an afterlife, yes; but *not* some kind of reward that can only come after this life has ended. He had a concept of a continuum, an uninterrupted connection between life here and now and life after death. Therefore, since this Kingdom is alive in us already, we can know the benefits of that Kingdom that bring real joy even in the midst of earthly persecution. This perception does not lead to a dead end, fatalistic kind of living, but to a life that always has meaning and purpose beyond the here and now.

The Aramaic people believed, as did most Middle Eastern people at the time, that the Creator reigns in very intimate presence to the cosmos seated above the firmament. Divine Providence therefore is not, as it were, coming from far away. In our contemporary way of thinking, we look to our sciences that are concrete and more understandable to us and we think give a more *scientifically* correct understanding of the earth and universe. We find it hard to take Jesus at his word about this Kingdom. Consequently, most of us just trudge through life without a sense of the full applicability of the truths Jesus speaks of. God is far away and science gives the answers we rely on.

Our only hope seems to be that if we are lucky, in the afterlife we will get to know what Jesus is talking about. In the meantime, we just pray with whitened knuckles that we are somehow on the right track with Jesus. Too many see the Beatitudes as admonitions to fulfill obligations in order to receive a reward in the afterlife, whereas Jesus is speaking of the reality of the Kingdom of God here and now. It does not help much if we can only expect to receive these gifts after the strife of life is over. That would be accepting suffering solely for the sake of ascetical values that supposedly lead to Heavenly rewards. Jesus knew there was no real practical help to people from such ways of thinking.

At the same time, Jesus does not teach "pie-in-the-sky" naiveté or Pharisee-like asceticism. He was a realist who saw reality from the point of view of the Kingdom of God. He had a realistic sense of the possibilities for the here and now in that context. Furthermore, he knew the Creator had greater things in mind for us than we usually imagine. It is to our detriment if we fail to accept the realism of Jesus because it does not fit our notions of how things work on the face of this earth. Our sciences do tell us how things work on the face of the earth, but not how things work in the Kingdom of the Beatitudes. Our scientific culture is manmade and as such is very fallible, whereas the wisdom of Jesus was from the Father. These Beatitudes are not man-made but are sure-fire prescriptions leading to the fullness of life Jesus so often spoke about and even promised.

Adversities of any kind take on a whole new meaning in the context of his Beatitude. Adversities are part and parcel with the pain of Creation coming into fullness. St. Paul says: "Creation groans and is in agony even unto now "(Romans, 8, 22). It is in agony because it has not yet come to its fullness, yet it does have a destiny of glory, the glory of the reign of God. So too do our own sufferings.

13

Earthly Secularity Ministers to Us

Secularity is defined by the dictionary as "human activity or things…not concerned with religion—not religious." Many are saying that our contemporary secular (material, worldly) culture has very negatively affected religion today. Now if religion and our contemporary secularity need tending to, we do well to begin with the earth and cosmos we inhabit and not to go searching for humanly contrived programs or research projects. People of many cultures and even earliest times did not find the material, secular earth to be a religious problem. It was the source of their faith and religious practices.

Just about everyone everywhere found Creation to be Creator oriented, that is, pointing to a Divine Creator. That being so, modern secular life need not necessarily be irreligious. Earth and all Creation will naturally lead to the Creator, though maybe not to any particular religion. However, there are a large number of contemporary people for whom religion has become irrelevant. Though it may not be objectively true, religion possibly seems too artificial for them, seemingly too manmade perhaps. Most of them are not running away from God, but from religious practices that seem meaningless.

To counteract what may seem to be meaningless in religious practice, the Church may need to give more explicit attention to the truth that the earthly foundations of the Church are in natural Creation where so many others have found God. The Graces of Sacrament and Liturgy administered by the church cannot be appreciated without reference to what is the natural bearer of those Graces. A more meaningful appreciation of our Creation roots could enhance an understanding of the Graced or Supernatural truths of Church life and practice. It is meaningless for most people to begin with the Supernatural. There is a maxim found in earliest theological writings that asserts: "The Supernatural builds on the natural," meaning to say, one does not or even cannot appreciate anything Supernatural without taking into account its natural foundations.

Before the compelling theological concepts that give meaning to Church practices can have any impact on the disaffected who are leaving the Church, there is need of more meaningful experiences of the *natural* in the Church, the likes of which moved even our more primitive forbearers to faith and religion. Primitive humankind had very little theology as we know it, but the Creator reached out to them just as they were, and they were able to respond in faith as the Creator had designed them to do. We are made to that same design and so can find the Creator from the same source—earth and cosmos. To this end, the Church might do well to realign more affectively and intellectually with earth and cosmos.

Possibly it is in our tendency to distance ourselves too much from the earth by our dependency on artificial contrivances where contemporary culture tends toward irreligion. We have come to the point where earth and cosmos cannot impact our lives in ways that were true of earlier humankind who lived in close proximity to all things natural. Part of a solution then may be for Churches to become more Creator-based especially in catechetical instructions.

And such instruction is easily done without a lot of complicated reasoning. Just the facts are all that is needed. The most basic truth is, the Church does not exist somehow above Creation but is integral to it because all members of the Churches are integral to Creation. All participants should be able to experience themselves Creation connected in church the same way many sense this connection when out in nature. Unfortunately, too many sense they are insulating themselves from nature and earth when they enter a church because they have been made to believe earth and nature may be beautiful but are not holy. The full truth is, anything that comes from the hands of the Creator is stamped with Divine beauty and goodness, and anything beautiful or inspiring is holy.

Part of the effort required from us in Religion and Church may then be to become more at one in thought and sentiment with earth and cosmos, to let nature be natural even in church. Does this mean we must regress to primitive religious practices? Actually that would be needless regression because God has been leading us to all the changes and advances we enjoy today; and the natural world we experience through our sciences is still the avenue to the Divine. That same world is our home and place of worship and prayer. If we facilitate an appreciation that the natural world around us and the natural elements incorporated in Sacrament and Liturgy are Sacred by their very nature, many may gain an appreciation of Church practices. Physical matter does not become holy and sacred because the Church blesses and uses them. They are holy and sacred by their created nature. At least for many, this sense of holiness is more captivating of mind and heart than the blessing of the church for objects and persons.

If the Church many are leaving can no longer hold them, perhaps simply reemphasizing the sacred earthiness of our religious practices may reclaim many of them. Everyone has a built-in capacity to respond to the Divine as experienced in the natural world. The more the sacred natural is expressed and accepted, and the more the artificial manmade takes second place, the more the Church might be experienced as God-directed verses human-directed. The human Jesus himself was of the earth, as is every human being born into this world; and he ministered to others as a fully human person ethnically and culturally formed by closeness to earth and cosmos. As he, so also the Church!

Furthermore, in a real way, secular earth and cosmos *ministered to* Jesus through his cultural and religious foundations. Through his Aramaic culture and Covenant Spirituality, earth and cosmos enriched his faith life. In the same way, our secular world today ministers to us, whether out in the world or in Church. Just as the Creator provided Divine guidance and Grace to earliest humankind through their primitive worship based on earth and cosmos, so does the Creator do it again through our contemporary religious structures.

Of course, it is the presence of the risen Lord in these Liturgical Rites that raises them above the primitive rites of ancient humankind, and even above the Old Testament practices. The risen Lord takes care of that just fine, but that transforming presence depends on our human Liturgical Rites and prayer to bring Church practitioners into meaningful interaction with the Lord. We are the hands of the risen Lord, but all this can remain irrelevant to the disaffected if we fail to reach them in ways that are meaningful to them in their contemporary cultural situation.

They are secular, that is, not religious in occupation, secular in the entire environment that envelops them; in contrast to the very ancient people who apparently recognized that their whole environment and even occupation were enveloped by the Divine. They sought and were able to interact with the Divine in the totality of their lives. Their lives and work were theocratic, that is, governed by the Creator. They had no church to teach or lead them in this; a Patriarch of a family or clan provided all the leadership they needed. Our contemporary social and Church structures facilitate our faith and religious journey in the same way, and can have the same faith-enlivening effects. So it is not just the Pope, Bishop, or Priest Celebrants that lead to God. It is the ever-abiding presence of the Creator who manifests himself to us through Creation and the risen Lord Jesus.

Perhaps instead of ministry to secularity, we should be speaking of the ministry of Creator-imbued secularity to us. So then, the way to reach and minister to those who are leaving established religion may be to let God do it God's way: through Creation. It bears repeating, we in the Catholic Church have already been set on that track in our Sacramental and Liturgical practices. We recognize Jesus with us especially in the bread and wine of the Eucharist and in all the Sacraments of the Church. There is a well-developed theology of Supernatural Grace, giving the Sacraments profound richness, but that theology will not be dealt with here. We will instead proceed with the theme of this chapter, natural secularity.

Each Sacrament builds on a natural quality of some material element or some human gesture that expresses what Jesus intended to do for people. Jesus himself knew the importance of such elements or gestures that conveyed his intent. His action to feed five thousand hungry people in an isolated location spoke to his intent to feed a deeper need that they and we have for Spiritual sustenance. Following that intent, for us today, a small bit of bread, and a sip of wine opens the recipient to the greater offering of that Spiritual food and drink that the risen Lord has become through his Sacramental presence in the bread and wine. Just as the Creator God gifts his material Creation with Divine sustaining Providence for humankind, so Jesus sustains his disciples by this Sacramental presence, and through that same material Creation.

With a frame of mind that recognizes that Divinely enriched Creation is fitting within the Church, many of the faithful participants may well experience the Church in a new light. Without detracting from the many other Spiritual gifts of the Church, we can also celebrate the natural. Theological explanations, true and necessary as they are, concern realities that are beyond our capacity to experience and for many to understand. This may well be why Jesus always referred to concrete human experiences that referred to otherworldly realities. He left them with real life experiences that led to, pointed to, were imbued with the Divine.

The Vatican II document: The *Church in the Modern World* speaks of this. In general, the Document says this world, this secularity manifests the presence of God and Jesus. The Church, more clearly acknowledging that it is at home in this secular Creation, will make it easy for us who are of this world to "fit" in, be at home in the Church, find commonality even with its complex structures. Then those who have shed its allegiance may find a home there again, and may then find that the Church, even in its human imperfections, is a blessing and nurturer of good things just as the earth itself nurtures life.

The presence of God will be as palpable and natural in church as out in nature. The Divine healing presence within the church may then be more clearly exemplified by the healing presence of earth and cosmos.

On the natural level, Church ministry will then be complementary to the ministry of Creation to humanity. On a higher level, the Sacramental ministry of the Church will more clearly manifest the ministry of Jesus himself. On the Sacramental and preaching level, the Church makes present the ministry of Jesus even more than Creation manifests the Creator. Jesus was made flesh from the substance of the earth as we all are and dwelt among us; and through his Resurrection to new life raised all humankind and thereby all Creation to a new level of unity with the Creator. Therefore, the ministry of the Church in its *most sublime role* is to make all things one in Christ—*through him, with him and in him,* and thereby one with the Creator.

Teilhard de Chardin, a French Jesuit paleontologist, philosopher, and cosmologist of the past century (1881-1955), "envisioned the graced capacity of humankind under the power of the Resurrection of Jesus to transform the world and its institutions and its work, its learning, its sciences. The late Popes, John Paul II and Pope Benedict XVI, have both been writing of the vocation of the Christian to transform the earth into a more livable place. This has particular application to our current worldwide economic and political predicament. Human creativity needs to be directed by fuller aspirations than improvements in material welfare alone because human beings are more and desire more, aesthetically, intellectually, ecologically, religiously. Ministry to the earth and to secularity is burgeoning beyond what humankind has usually thought" (cf. an article in *America* magazine, Aug. 17, 2009, Teilhard at Vespers).

To further this reflection, consider how the Holy Spirit interacted with the disciples on Pentecost. The presence of the risen Lord is *the* defining reality of the Church; but the *physical experience* of Pentecost was of *fire and roaring winds*; and it must have been a very stunning and dramatic experience. Even though what gave that experience its real potency was the presence of the Spirit of the risen Lord, and as important and enlivening as eventual theological explanations of this event were, it was the fire and wind that opened them to the Holy Spirit.

Theological explanations always enrich the experiences of the Church, but there could have been no theology of Pentecost without the earthly experience of fire and wind. In the same way, earth and cosmos are the defining experiences of the Creator. Without earth and all Creation we can never know, experience, or celebrate the Divine Creator. Surely, this should encourage us to let Creator-enriched secularity minister to us in this crisis time of the Church. Then secularity will not be a problem but an asset.

Jesus of Nazareth was of the earth as we are also; and even after his Resurrection he remains earth-based through the Sacraments. He said he would always be with us and we would be doing even greater things than he did. After the Resurrection, the risen Lord said, "With me all things (even those greater things) are possible," and it would seem this implies that we remain as earth-based as Jesus of the Gospels had been. That is who he was, that is who we are. We today need to experience the presence of the Holy Spirit in our natural surroundings in order to enhance our experience of the Supernatural in our gathering in community for prayer and Sacrament.

What is needed is not change in the Church's theology or practices, but changes in our mindset that supposes the natural is a distraction from the more important purposes of the Church. We need to trust that God knows our design much better than we do, and has been successful in reaching out to humankind in God's own-way—through Creation. Even God's Word made flesh in the person of Jesus of Nazareth is "nature-made," born of the Virgin Mary, and walked the face of the earth and taught his truths through references to all things of the earth. He suffered death and was enclosed in a sepulcher in the earth, only to rise to a new life that enriches all of Creation; and thus once more, physical Creation (the earth and sepulcher) are the vehicles of God's saving work. The Creator is consistent and easy to comprehend in his physical works; and is a better guide to worship and prayer than sometimes complicated human ways.

14

For Lack of Attention to Creation-Centeredness, the Church is Losing the Disappointed and Uninterested

Many things are contributing to the mounting exodus of churchgoers from their places of worship, precipitating many surveys and guesses and some conclusions. This chapter will suggest one possible source of discontent among those leaving, though maybe not the most prominent, yet possibly significant. This chapter will not deal with either the meaning or structure of Liturgy, nor with the manner of presiding; but rather will suggest that the lack of attention given to Creation and to the Creator in the usual *catechesis* about Liturgical celebration is where some fault may lie. To bring about changes needed today would not entail wholesale changes as took place after Vatican II in the mid-sixties, but mostly a change in *mindset.*

The Creator is most impressively evident to us through physical Creation, and to ignore Creation is to disregard the Creator. In Liturgy this deficit becomes particularly significant. While it is true the risen Lord is the central person celebrated in Liturgy, it may prove helpful to review the place of physical Creation in Ecclesial Liturgy, and to assess the negative effect on parish Liturgical Life this neglect may be having. Perhaps it is because of our *rightful* attention to the place of the risen Lord in prayer and worship, that it has escaped us that Jesus himself was based in his own faith and in his teachings on the cosmos, the Creator, and on our reliance on the earth.

Sacred Religious Rites and Rituals of Liturgy did not rise up to mind and practice out of a vacuum; nor do they arise out of rational efforts alone. They are based as well on deep intuitive sensitivities. Our souls, our spirits, are very active within us in ways our minds do not recognize all the time, yet in ways that affect us very much. We are actually aware in this way of Creation's own liturgies—the regular cycles of daily and monthly movements of moon and sun, seasonal cycles, and nature's own ongoing evolution. The Creator himself initiated these great moments and movements within the universe; and every time we pass through these cycles we celebrate those liturgies with the Creator. The rites of our Church Liturgies are in some ways patterned on those Creation Liturgies, although Ecclesial Liturgies celebrate great moments and movements in Divine Salvation history. Both of these Liturgies move us along the journey of Creation coming to fulfillment.

Liturgies that accentuate our ties to earth and cosmos cannot help but grab our sensitivities whether we are conscious of it or not, because earth and cosmos reverberate throughout our very physical make up. That may be why the material matter of the Sacraments, as simple as they are, has the capacity to touch us in simple but moving ways. When we let nature be natural in Sacramental and Liturgical practices, the Creator comes through much more authentically and the magnificence of the Creator himself reflected in our natural surroundings.

Physical Creation by its very nature draws faith-filled individuals to want to celebrate the existence of the Creator in the beauty and grandeur of nature. For those who go out of doors and experience nature in its changing seasons, its lavish, extravagant landscapes, and varied sensual experiences, their whole being can be engaged not only with nature but more importantly with the Creator himself. The Liturgy of the Church can and needs to be engaged with all this physical and spiritual richness in order to draw participants along to the fullness of faith; and to ignore that in Liturgy deprives it of the full faith-enriching potential it could have.

For lack of significant affective enrichment that Creation could contribute, Liturgy for many is nothing more than prescribed prayers and songs; and what ought to hold members together in hallowed and empowering communion, may be contributing to their exodus. So the question needs to be asked, just what might constitute a richer experience on that human/creational level that could hold some of those who are leaving? What might they instinctively be looking for? Given the fact that for many there is nothing more inspiring and compelling than Creation physically experienced, it just might be that many of the faithful are instinctively longing for more profound religious experiences of Creation and of the Creator.

Creation and the Creator could easily and more clearly be celebrated in Liturgy than is the practice now. While Liturgical decor often does include items brought in from the out of doors—tree branches, flowers and other items that are judicially and thoughtfully displayed—parishioners must know from ongoing instructions that this serves more than just to decorate the church. There needs to be an understanding that it all signifies our individual and Ecclesial grounding in Creation. Creation out in nature is before our eyes all the time, so nature and Liturgy naturally commingle.

Faith-fortified observers of the natural world will naturally want to celebrate the Divine Creator because it is a built-in impulse. It fulfills our very nature as creatures of God. The failure to more distinctly acknowledge and celebrate the Creator and Creation in Liturgy may possibly contribute to a not clearly defined sense of dissatisfaction in some. Spiritual realities for many are difficult to articulate, especially concerning what might be lacking in religious experiences; but a finely nuanced Liturgical experience may make a big difference for many of the discontented.

Weak and trifling approaches to the Divine in prayer and worship are likely to leave many people disappointed and uninterested. If the experience of the Divine in church is less inspiring than can be experienced out in nature or in musical and other artistic presentations, significant numbers may well lose interest. For the average contemporary person, good experiences are more important than intellectual explanations. If it is not experienced as worthwhile, all the theological explanations of how it should be evaluated will not count for much. We live in a good experience-demanding age, and not too surprisingly, creation provides just that.

To bring about these enhanced experiences, nothing need be changed in the design of our official Liturgies, but through early education and ongoing adult explanations, an appreciation of Creation's place in Liturgy could easily be encouraged. It would not take elaborate theological explanations to provide the background for this understanding.

Participants in Church life, whether Liturgical or Sacramental, do not necessarily need copious displays of nature, but an understanding of the significance of ourselves as part and parcel of Creation. Most may well be powerfully aware of the universe as it is being put before us by contemporary science, but science as science cannot put us in touch with the Creator and all the awesome significance of Creation itself. Only the Creator can draw us into communion with himself through the medium of Creation, and especially fortified through the medium of Sacrament and Liturgy.

15

Sacraments are Earthly Signs for an Earthly People

The birth of Jesus of Nazareth is the beginning of new life not only for the son of Mary, but for all of humankind. It has been called the beginning of a new Creation. First Creation can be observed all across and within the earth we occupy, and throughout the far reaches of the physical universe all around us. The new Creation can be observed in the life and teaching of Jesus of Nazareth, the son of Mary and (supposedly) Joseph as he walked across the face of the earth. This new Creation was totally accessible as a neighbor, friend, and companion. Through those personal relationships he eventually brought the healing love necessary to begin the restoration of full human life and the restoration of the integrity of Creation disrupted by the sin.

He began his ministry by gathering a band of twelve Apostles who accompanied him everywhere for three years, listening, learning, but most importantly, observing how he interacted in a healing way with people in their many different needs. This little band of disciples no doubt enjoyed this time with him and learned much, but they soon encountered many people and situations working against them, especially in the person of overzealous Pharisees and Temple authorities. The cohesive glue, as it were, that held them together in spite of the internal and external forces that could have torn them apart, was the person of Jesus.

From the perspective of over two millennia now, we the much larger band of disciples can catch something from the words and deeds of Jesus of Nazareth that those earlier disciples could not fully appreciate at the time. There were many indications that his life and teachings were not going to be commonplace. This was poignantly exemplified when Jesus promised he would be giving them food of greater value than ordinary food, and this food that he would give was his own flesh and blood that would bring them everlasting life. Not your ordinary way of talking by any reckoning.

It is not too surprising that many found these words hard to comprehend, and in fact, many discontinued listening to him after that. But when he asked the Apostles if they were going to leave him too, Peter answered, "To whom shall we go, you have the words of everlasting life" (Jn. 6, 53-69). It seemed a group decision by the Apostles that Jesus was their best bet. Many, many times thereafter it was the attraction of who Jesus was that kept them together. He was no common ordinary person, maybe not what most expected, but definitely someone worth paying attention to; and most of them remained faithfully with him to a bitter end.

He was able to keep his little band of Apostles together by the power of his presence with them. They slowly came to a realization that there was much more to this man Jesus than first met the eye. Mystery upon mystery accumulated through the three years they spent with him. Fortunately, he promised he would remain with them forever, and they came to appreciate that if he said it, he would probably do just that. All this culminated in an experience that would change their lives forever—his Resurrection to a new life. It took a while before the consequences of the Resurrection would begin to bear fruit in their own lives and in the communities that began to gather in memory of him.

Later on, after Jesus had ascended to his Glory and his disciples began gathering in his name, the opposition forces got even worse. The Romans persecuted them because they would not pledge allegiance to the Emperor, and used their typical violent tactics to suppress them. The Pharisees and Temple authorities also kept up ever-increasing opposition. The only way these disciples could hope to remain faithful to the directive of Jesus to spread his message everywhere would be by taking strength from their experience of his continued presence with them. Fortunately, they found that his promise to remain with them really did come to fruition after his Resurrection from the dead.

Beginning with his surprising presence with them in their prayerful rite of "Breaking of the Bread" that they celebrated in memory of him, his presence became ever more enriching. As they did their best to continue the ministries that exemplified his life and teachings, they found themselves empowered by that presence in many momentous ways. Under the inspiration of his abiding Spirit, they began devising memorial prayer rituals to help them in various ministries they continued in memory of him.

It would have been natural to utilize in these prayer rites the same earthly substances along with the very words of Jesus that were associated with certain ministries he did. Jesus consistently included references in his teachings to the earth and to earthly matters familiar to everyone, so natural elements would have come to mind when they wanted to shape memorial rites and rituals. Reference to earth and cosmos were not just imaginative linguistic devises in that Aramaic culture, but they were realities that profoundly affected their lives. That is why the earth and universe-centered parables of Jesus were so powerful for them. Naturally, the disciples would continue in this earthly vein.

Eventually, individual Churches devised their own unique practices in order to keep alive the many different types of ministries Jesus had done. In the very beginning, the number of these rites and rituals was limited only to what they could remember Jesus doing, so the numbers of the rites were probably in the dozens. Eventually as they began building structures specifically for their gatherings, the rites took on more formal and standardized forms. Slowly, after several generations, the seven rites we call the Sacraments were finalized. Through these rituals and other prayer rites, a living relationship with the risen Lord has been maintained.

The Hebrew people, who were of course the first Christians, always felt themselves also deeply committed to and engaged in "Old Covenant Law and practices. Therefore for some time, the Christian communities considered themselves observant Jews. They felt no need to give all that up. Unfortunately, the Temple authorities eventually expelled them from Synagogue and Temple as heretics; but Christian Jews could live with the satisfaction that they were one with Jesus the High Priest of a new Covenant (cf. Heb chapters 7 & 8).

In time, the realization dawned among them that the new Covenant in the Blood of the Lamb of God, that is, the Crucified Christ, fulfilled the Old Covenant and brought it to a fitting and glorious fulfillment. Once they came to sense the full truth of this, their prayer and ministry took on a completely new meaning. Though they remained immersed in their cultural and Old Covenant grounding, it all took on new life and significance. The Old Covenant that had been maintained by mostly symbolic rites found fulfillment and satisfaction in a new reality, the reality of their new life in the risen Lord.

Of course, it goes without saying that even today we partake in that same ongoing salvation history begun in the Old Testament and continued in the life and deeds of Jesus of Nazareth and in the Ritual remembrances of the early Church. That is what makes our individual lives, our parishes, our families, and the worldwide Christian community so extraordinary; it is because we partake in the Resurrected life of Jesus. He is the one who holds us together and continues his life and ministry through us. This reality of Resurrection Life finds its sustenance in these same rites we today call the seven Sacraments. That number seven is not important as is the reality of the presence of the

Risen Lord in our Parishes and Dioceses. Those seven Sacraments do maintain in real time the very ministries of Jesus of Nazareth.

As in the Gospel days, so now we probably could not maintain our identity as Disciples of Jesus without this abiding presence. And without this presence the healing ministries of Jesus would not continue. Jesus himself took consolation knowing he was fulfilling the Prophesies of old that predicted the coming Messiah would bring healing to a suffering people.

Consequently, the Mystical Body of Christ, the Church today, cannot claim fellowship with Jesus the Risen Lord unless it is genuinely healing in all its works and manifestations. Each of the seven Sacraments contributes to that overall ministry of healing to a suffering world. If the Church is not recognized as genuinely healing but instead actually inflicts pain from unyielding demands of obedience and compliance to teachings, it will not be respected, nor can it be fully effective in the ministries it attempts.

16

Baptism—Creation-Encompassing, Life-Giving—Water

To understand why water is the element or sign of the Sacrament of Baptism we need take note first that Jesus himself was baptized by John the Baptist in the river Jordan (Mk 1, 9). However, that fact does not begin to exhaust the natural and Spiritual significance of the Waters of Baptism.

Water was and still is the universal element used for cleansing, which may have been why John and others baptized their prospective followers by immersion in water. Physical cleansing by water signified a desire to be cleansed of sin and adhere to the teachings of the teacher. However, the element of water carries even more significance. No matter the religion or culture, water carries deeply Spiritual significance, based on water's natural physical uses and importance for life.

Though we moderns live greatly insulated from earth and nature, water still possess a deep down instinctive meaning. It is innate to us because of our physical roots in the formation processes of the earth brought about partly by the powerful effects of water; and even more importantly, it constitutes a lot of our own physical makeup. We are earthly to the core of our being. Consequently, artificially contrived objects and forces have less deep down pull on us than the natural even though we have been conditioned to prefer what is manufactured.

It has been a known fact for a long time that we lived in a sack of water for nine months in the womb of our mothers where water contributed to our physical being. We are no strangers to water. And beyond that primal effect of water, we can take note of so many manifestations of water that enrich our lives——deserts spring to life after a rainfall; a garden newly planted begins to sprout from the seeds put in the ground; farmers who have invested significant amounts of money in seed, hoping for a harvest later that fall, feel tremendous relief and a surge of joy when the first rain falls on the field; and even a houseplant that may have begun to wilt from a momentary lack of water due to forgetfulness, revives with a generous dose of water. Or consider your experience of standing transfixed before a waterfall, listened to a small stream tinkle over the rocky bottom, or listened to a large river roar over a dam, or watching a heavy downfall of rain. One could go one almost endlessly naming those life-giving experiences of water.

And above and beyond these effects of water presently experienced, who has not stood in awe before the evidence of what water has done to the earth over time? Erosion of river beds that contributed to such wonder as the Grand Canyon, broad valleys with the river that made them still flowing and making everything green and lush. Water is so precious that we try to measure each rainfall, yet the volumes of water in lakes, rivers, and the oceans are measureless.

It is such fullness of meaning that is needed to help us appreciate the sign value of the waters of Baptism. Just as life cannot be appreciated from a momentary glance at a few living things, so too the life-giving Waters of Baptism cannot be appreciated from a few prosaic descriptions. It takes the best of poetic expressions, song, art, and science to plumb the depth of the meaning of the Waters of Baptism. Baptism then is so much more than what meets the eye, and being initiated into the Church in fellowship with the Risen Lord through Baptism is so much more than what meets the eye.

To appreciate the Sacrament of Baptism in a way that makes it more than a simple action of pouring water, to inspire parents and neophytes to the Church to be open to the astounding Graces of that rite needs a profound appreciation of water. The theology of Baptism will not mean much without a thorough grounding in the natural bearer of the Grace of the Sacrament, water.

Also of profound significance, we must be attentive to the deeply moving effect Jesus likely experienced as he stepped into the Jordan River for his own Baptism. The waters of the River Jordan already had centuries of accumulated significance for the Hebrew people. That river baptism experience opened Jesus to the voice of the Father affirming him as his beloved son. That Baptism experience of Jesus was the bridge between the Old Law and the New Covenant originated by Jesus on the Cross. Natural Creation is bridged to the new Creation instigated by Jesus through those waters of the Jordan.

The child or adult at their Baptism is Spiritually enveloped in all this. The little candle given to the parents or sponsor of the one being Baptized signifies the much more awesome light that bathes the child or adult at that moment of Baptism. That little light is evocative of the blast of light that initiated Creation's physical beginnings. The glory of the Divine Realm from which all this originated is so far above us we do well not to try to equal it. A flickering candle does it just fine.

That water and that light signify that we are affirmed by the Father as beloved, just as Jesus had experienced it. Baptism is as awesome as all that, and it is as cosmic in its primal grounding as is water. Water calls up even more primal realities than *earthbound* processes. Water is *cosmic* in scope, Creation encompassing. It is significant that Baptism is called entry into a New Life. It is no small thing to be born into natural life on this earth; and it is no small thing to be Baptized with Creation's most life-giving element—water.

One final consideration: Water can kill by drowning. The water of Baptism signifies dying to one's old self so a new self can emerge. The Spiritual death of Baptism is as awesome as the extraterrestrial death of stars that contemporary science describes where a completely new stellar structure emerges from such a cosmic event. Yet even more astounding is the birth to new life in Baptism. A whole new Creation emerges from the death of Baptism. The Body of Christ, the Church, is brought to life to the glory of God and the Salvation of humankind. Neither quasars nor black holes nor dark matter out in the far reaches of the universe equal in awesome magnitude this new life in the Resurrection of Jesus. All Creation has come full circle so the Creator's plan envisioned from the beginning of time finds fulfillment in the waters of Baptism. Baptism is of no small consequence because it is of Creation proportions.

17

Confirmed for Discipleship, Anointed with Dignity

Probably everyone has experienced feeling inadequate to a task or a trying situation. A feeling of intellectual inadequacy and worn out resolve can spread through one's whole being and negative thoughts may plague us. But sometimes there may also be an undefined sense of an inner strength. It is unfortunate, though, that we usually give the most attention to the conscious negative thoughts and feelings, while the real inner strength within us lays dormant, awaiting some event or person to enliven it.

It would seem Jesus had a sense of his own inner strength, and he trusted that each and every one of the people he dealt with possessed these inner qualities that may have been wounded by sin or weakened by overwhelming cultural influences. His ministries quite often were intended to empower them with hope and confidence that they were basically good and were blessed by Yahweh. To know that one is blessed by God is healing and strengthening especially for those who have been led to believe they were inferior or maybe even cursed by God. In those days, sickness was believed to be a sign of God's displeasure.

Both the Old Testament and New Testament attest to these debilitating notions about sickness. In fact, the Gospel writers always say Jesus was driving out evil spirits when he healed someone. And so, many healing stories recorded in the Gospels may have been Confirmation-like stories. Jesus was confirming them in their basic goodness by the healing.

The entire three years that Jesus' Apostles followed him, listening to his instruction, gaining wise counseling and guidance were what we today might call Confirmation preparation. They discovered that his teachings gave new life to old beliefs, correction to misguided opinions, avenues to more meaningful reflections, insights into Divinely inspired wisdom. One can be sure he spent extra time also discussing with them the imagery and the meaning of his parables about planting seed and harvesting crops, and would also have reflected further with them about the awesome giftedness of earth and cosmos. He enriched their natural cultural appreciation of earth and cosmos so it helped them draw even closer to the enriching realm of the Creator.

They needed to be fortified by a share of the inner strength Jesus manifested. They would need all that to face the difficult tasks that awaited them as active disciples. One can guess those Apostles got a lot of that enrichment by observing Jesus at prayer with the Father and by joining him in prayer. They followed him in regular attendance at the Synagogue for formal Scripture reading, song, and instruction from respected elders. This kept them attuned to the Covenant Law from which Jesus himself drew Spiritual strength.

Probably most people recognized that Jesus had more to offer than good advice or encouragement. He was a source of empowerment to those lacking inner strength or personal initiative. He confirmed individuals, young and old, in an appreciation of their basic humanness, helping them reestablish a weakened faith and hope. This was not miraculous in any way but it was Spiritually empowering for a more beneficial life.

Later on, during the formative times of the Church, the Apostles surely would have reminisced and told stories about those days spent in close association with him and all the benefits they gained from this relationship. As they continued to experience his abiding presence with them, this presence surely proved to be a crucial source of Spiritual strength. Saint Paul who was legendary even before his writings gained wide attention, often spoke of the presence of the Lord as *his* source of strength. Stories coming in from the far-flung regions where Paul ministered told of pagan converts also experiencing this presence.

Eventually, they must have come to the conclusion that some kind of memorializing of this source of fortitude could prove to be valuable. As always, the question arose, how to visibly signify that particular gift. Memories of how Jesus himself used earthly materials to emphasize his intent for a recipient, often suggested by Old Law practices, gave them rich resources to draw from. Certain materials are naturals for symbolic purposes, and one can load them with a lot.

All natural elements have their origins in the earliest stages of the Creation process where they were impacted by energies and forces beyond what we can even imagine. Even our physical and affective selves draw from that energy because our bodies are composed of those same physical particles now also part and parcel with the earth. The earth and its myriads of growing processes, along with the healing potentials of minerals and plants used in those ancient times were mysterious yet powerful. They did not need our contemporary scientific explanations to reap many of the spiritual benefits of nature. Sometimes the affective and Spiritual potency of physical materials are more powerful than scientific knowledge and applications, which quite likely explains why traditional home remedies were often quite effective.

Oil applied to wounds for healing and rubbed on the bodies of athletes as a strengthening measure would not have those qualities unless they shared in the Creator's own vitality. Neither would contemporary medical applications of nature's substances have their effect unless they shared in that same vitality. Aramaics and many other cultures were in tune with many of these natural realities and insightfully attributed it to Divine/Creational potency. Anointing with oil today in the Sacrament of Confirmation, though not physically medicinal, carries all these significances and Creation potentials.

And yet, that is hardly the sum of it. There is also the long-standing practice of anointing Kings and Prophets with oil, signifying dignity and authority. Prophets and Old Testament Kings being anointed for their roles always seemed to experience Divine empowerment. If we cannot associate our contemporary Sacramental Confirmation with an empowering dignity, we may be missing something very important for Confirmation candidates today. Acceptance of the call to mature discipleship with Jesus certainly implies a dignity. Without recognition of that dignity that goes with discipleship, the young may not be stimulated for the responsibilities.

This blessing and anointing of Confirmation candidates signifies an important moment in the life of individual Christians and Christian communities. It is a moment of decision for the candidate and of election by Jesus to be a disciple. It is no small thing to be elected by Jesus as a disciple and anointed by the Holy Spirit. The flaming-fire and wind-blowing potency of Pentecost is alive there. We are called Christian because we are Disciples "in the risen Lord," as Saint Paul would say it. The Sacrament of Confirmation facilitates the ministry of the risen Lord for these candidates.

The Oil of Confirmation confers the commissioning of a Disciple of the Risen Christ to fill out the effective ministerial role of the Mystical Body of Christ. Even though the human mind may not be able to name the experience this way, the very glorious energy of the Resurrection shines through. Physically it is Creation activated; Spiritually it is Holy Spirit activated; Ecclesiastically it is Sacramentally activated.

77

18

Bread and Wine Vitalized to Nourish New Life

The first act of Creation and the succeeding timeless processes of evolving elements and components of productive earthen fields eventually culminated in the making of bread and wine for nutritional and celebrative purposes. Probably no one spends much time reflecting on that timeless process, but there are countless individuals who spend innumerable moments enjoying the sight, aroma, and taste of bread and wine. Bread and wine are iconic, symbolizing food, nourishment, and tasteful gratification.

However, that is not the end of the saga of bread and wine. Jesus of Nazareth took that one impressive step further, saying he would always be present with those who shared a loaf of bread and a cup of wine in ritual memory of him. That bread, he said, was truly his body, and the wine was truly his blood that he offered as a Sacrifice on the Cross. This is truly an extraordinary addition to the significance of bread and wine.

That final stage of this unfolding chronicle took place on the night of the Last Supper, when Jesus did and said things that could only be comprehended over time. As a noteworthy addition to that final Passover Seder meal where Jesus presided, he first did an unexpected thing by washing the feet of his disciples. They always knew Jesus was not into insignificant and ineffectual little gestures, so they knew by that foot washing they were called together in that Ritual meal in order to go out and serve others. Moreover, something greater than memorializing the eventful journey of the Hebrew Nation through the desolate desert is inaugurated that evening. The very journey of Creation to its fulfillment takes a big step here.

That simple and humble gesture of washing the feet of his disciples as well as the rest of that mystifying meal probably stretched all their emotional and

rational sensibilities, but eventually after the Resurrection, they came to realize the full meaning of that meal, that foot washing. While they always
knew they could take Jesus at his word, even though at times what he did
and said was mystifying, they would not grasp the full meaning of that Seder
meal until Jesus rose from the dead and appeared among them in numerous
illuminating situations.

Over time they came to understand they were called to a Spiritual transformation of much greater proportions than their nation had been called to in
their Old Covenant with Yahweh. This Passover celebration of a new and everlasting Covenant in the blood of Jesus was not just a replication of the old rite,
but was the completion of a progression of Creation events bringing not only
their nation but all people of all times to the full life the Creator intended from
the beginning of Creation. Divine inspired events are always Creation-wide
in scope and meaning.

The traditional Passover celebrations were always memorable because of
the significance of the Exodus event alluded to in that annual celebration. The
troublesome and dangerous, long, drawn-out journey through an arid land instigated a most profound Spiritual experience for the people. Over time under
the guidance of Moses the Covenant maker, and after him with the help of
many great Prophets, they came to associate that physical journey from slavery
in Egypt to freedom in their Promised Land with a much more profound Spiritual and Religious transformation to which they were called. But the New
Covenant journey, they would soon learn, was empowered by the Resurrection
of Jesus, an event even greater than the experience of Moses on Mount Sinai.

From the Resurrection of Jesus came the new life to which he had been
calling them. From that new life comes transforming energy and Grace with
all the vigor and power of Creation's beginnings. Soon Pentecost would give
them the fire and energy of the Spirit to enliven their journey. They would be
Confirmed in roaring wind and raging fire and become a beacon of light to
the world, a leaven in the sinful culture of the world the same way Jesus had
been. This is intended to be a new Creation, a new beginning.

Through that Seder celebration, their whole concept of Covenant Life
and practice was raised to a completely new level. Over time, so many things
Jesus had said and done began to come together and the picture that began to
emerge was transformational. The Eucharist, as it came to be called, was to
be the centerpiece, the most consequential Covenantal celebration. The Eucharist would be the heart of the new Covenant Community, giving meaning
and cohesion to all their ritual celebrations (Sacraments) just as Jesus himself
had been in the Gospel days. The Eucharist would be the life's blood for the
Mystical Body of Christ, just as the blood of Jesus on the Cross had been. From

here the Risen Lord of the Resurrection would continue the work of transforming cultures, nations, and all humankind for life in the Kingdom of God. From here the promise of Jesus to be with his disciples until the end of time would find its fulfillment. From here Creation itself would find its realization.

19

Sin and Healing Forgiveness

One of the consequences of sin is the disfigurement of the Creator's original handiwork. It is often noted that sin leaves a wound on the sinner as well as on others affected by sin. However, it is not only human persons that are wounded but also the earth, our home. God's Creation, especially the earth, was designed to support life; but human life on this earth is all too often curtailed and disfigured by sin. Jesus said he had come that we might have life to the fullest as the Creator intended us to have, and therefore a major portion of his ministry included healing the wounds of sin.

Despite a collective longing for forgiveness and its healing, forgiveness was not easy to come by in the religious climate of the time when Jesus began his ministry. The reform-minded Pharisees trying to restore the religious practices of the Covenant went overboard and created a scrupulous-minded attention to details so that everyone was easily and often judged guilty of religious and moral transgressions. Everyone was labeled good guys or bad guys and was treated accordingly. This of course led to a lot of hypocrisy and grandstanding; you hid the sin and advertised the positive. This attitude of the Pharisees troubled Jesus very much, and as a consequence of going against their teachings, found himself in serious and dangerous conflict with them.

The words and stories of Jesus, on the other hand, told of forgiveness and conveyed a healing balm for those suffering people so that many probably jostled for a position near him, to talk with him, or even just listen. The God Jesus prayed to and talked about was not the God so many had been led to believe in. The Father to whom Jesus prayed and referred to so often was truly a healing God. In one sense, Jesus could not help but be a healer. Yet he was able do this *not* because he was the Son of God, but because as the human son of Mary, he was open to the love of the Father who longs to renew his Creation. Jesus was a vehicle of that healing love. It deserves repeating here, all great happenings are Creation-centered, as were the ministries of Jesus.

Matters did not go well for the early Jewish Christian communities forming to live out the New Covenant. They were treated very harshly and unfairly by the Jewish authorities. The Temple authorities expelled this Christian sect from the Temple and Synagogue because they were considered heretics. On top of this, the Roman authorities considered them disloyal because they would not worship the Emperor; and eventually began very severe and unjust persecutions. The first generations of faithful Disciples suffered much from this two-pronged offensive. *They had much they needed to forgive.*

One can imagine them gathering in prayer and discussion about all these injustices done to them. At the same time, they certainly recalled the many teachings of Jesus on forgiveness, and maybe in the process of this remembrance and prayer, his forgiving presence with them became actually palpable. It is easy also to visualize the peace and joy and healing they experienced in this presence. Just as with the "Breaking of the Bread" gatherings where they recognized his presence with them, they longed to memorialize that healing forgiveness also.

This would have prompted the early Church to structure a prayer service furthering a ministry of healing forgiveness. They certainly recognized they had a pattern for this rite of forgiveness in many of the stories and forgiving examples of Jesus—the sinful women caught in adultery; the woman at the well; the thief who hung on a cross beside him; Peter, Judas and all the Apostles at one time or another. They must have remembered how people flocked to listen to him and how many went away renewed in faith and healing. That may well have been a personal experience for many of those disciples. A prayer gathering seeking strength to endure the painful injustices toward them could well have been one of the early rites of remembrance.

As they developed a Rite of Reconciliation, they surely recognized that sin always affects the community no matter how private sins may be, so the rites were designed to bring about reconciliation within the community as well. It was not for nothing that many of their Jewish and pagan neighbors said: whatever else you might say about some of their weird practices, "see how those followers of Jesus love one another."

The words of Absolution proclaimed today in Sacramental Reconciliation carry all the same healing potential of the words of Jesus. Both Penitent and Confessor are furthering the curative potential of a much needed Grace Both Penitent and Confessor of the Sacrament are involved in Creationwide happenings, initiated by the earthly ministry of Jesus of Nazareth. If we pay heed to it, no matter how we come to reconciliation, it always stirs the soul. The Sacrament of Reconciliation is a healing Sacrament intended to affect the soul not only of individuals but of families and communities—even the world itself.

Perhaps a renewed appreciation of this much broader communal aspect of the Sacrament of Reconciliation could instigate a renewal of the Sacrament so many long for. But this renewal will require a renewed sense of its place in the scheme of Creation. It has been a theme of this book that everything does fit in that scheme, and in fact so many things within the Church as well as in the world at large are awaiting just such an awakening to the reality of Creation.

So many unpeaceable, disruptive, and dangerous situations will always seem to be intractable. So many peace-searching things are constantly being tried: so-called policing wars, punishing sanctions, punitive incarcerations, and sometimes just letting the protagonist stew in their troubles. It is pretty hard to find any of that in the Gospels of Jesus of Nazareth, but reference to Creation in its many forms is a constant.

And some might say look where it got him. Why have we not paid more attention to just what he did accomplish? He did not cause any disturbance; he did not even bend a reed in a swamp. He did not add to any problem, which is more than can be said of humankind ever since. Do no harm because any harm only causes more harm! From his instrument of execution, the Cross, at the moment the world was being blessed with Redemption, he said: "Father, forgive them for they do not know what they are doing." Yes, we are forgiven. Obviously he expects us to start from there. From where else can we start?

That is where the Sacrament of Reconciliation starts: we are already forgiven, but we desperately need to open ourselves to the healing of Jesus being administered to us in the Sacrament. Sacramental Penances are not punishments but prayers for healing and for enlightenment to understand the full extent of our sins. Until we understand what we have done to mar Creation by our sins, our pledge to amend our ways will be ineffectual. This much maligned and neglected Sacrament needs a deeper understanding of the scope of sin as well as an understanding of just what Jesus intends for us, before any real individual or communal renewal can take place. Jesus was known to be a healer for a good reason—he wanted to be a healer. If then, why not today? We can be healers for one another and for the earth only when we understand just what our own healing forgiveness entails.

20

Freed from Two Misguided Notions of Sickness

The first mistaken notion of sickness was found among the contemporaries of Jesus of Nazareth. Their mistake was not medical in nature but it was their assumption that sickness had a Divine source. The common belief was that anyone suffering from a sickness or disability was being punished by God for some misdeed committed either by themselves or someone in his or her family. It is not hard to imagine the double distress this caused the sick ones.

Physical sickness and disabilities or the fear of those possibilities was a constant factor in the lives of most people in those Biblical times. Consequently, attention to the sick and disabled occupied a lot of the time of Jesus of Nazareth. He was deeply and genuinely mindful of what other people were experiencing and was well aware of the prevailing notion that God was the punisher of those who they were sick or suffering some tragedy. Jesus not only gave them the assurance God did *not* do that to them, but opened them in some deep way to what God really wanted to do for them. He was giving them a completely new vision of what God is like to these people. Our God-concept affects our lives more than we probably realize.

Most of the healings attributed to Jesus probably were not dramatic, nor were they all miraculous, though some no doubt were both. Jesus took pains not to get the reputation as a miracle worker, yet he definitely did want to be a healer partly because he knew so many needed it, and possibly also because he sensed it was significant for his ministry. On one occasion some skeptical Jewish authorities asked what sign he could give that his ministry was from God, and his response was, "Notice what is happening when I go about among people; the blind recover their sight, cripples walk, lepers are cured, the deaf

84

hear, dead men are raised to life, and the poor have the good news preached to them." (Mt 11, 5). Jesus was saying his healing ministry was the fulfillment of ancient prophesies they all recognized as pertaining to the future Messiah.

This was meant to assure those people that his ministry to the sick was from God. While it must have given him great satisfaction that he was able to help so many people, this Scripture passage may also have given verification to himself that his ministry actually fit the Prophetic expectations. He most certainly remembered the affirmation he heard at his baptism at the River Jordan before he began his public ministry. It was a powerful affirmation to know he was beloved by the Father (Mk 1, 9-11) and to have this further validation that his ministry of healing was doing the will of the Father added to his self-assurance. This affirmation also helps us even today to go deeper into the meaning of his healing ministry.

To go deeper we need go wider and consider his ministry in relation to Creation. From the perspective of Creation, Jesus was the pinnacle of the Creator's work. He was not only the one about whom the O.T. Prophets prophesied, but the one Creation had been waiting for since time immemorial. This Cosmic Christ had his human roots in the earth because he came into the world born of a woman; suffered death on a cross, the victim of human malice; and rose to new life escaping from a sepulcher in the earth. And finally, in the Church today he ministers to us through earthly Sacramental signs and symbols. He is one with us in every human and earthly way.

All Creation suffers from the sins and disastrous deeds of humankind because the intent of Creation is frustrated in its basic purpose to facilitate life. When a baby has a troublesome sickness, Creation is able to counter the sickness by providing basic ingredients for healing from the elements of the earth. Even contemporary medicines used by doctors depend to a great extent on the natural curative effects of plants and natural elements, which to people of faith is a manifestation of Divine Providence. Humankind always does best when working in concurrence with the earth and Creation, as when natural science is pursued for the benefit of humankind. The healing ministry of Jesus was earth- and Creation-centered, though usually not medicinal. His intent was to show the gracious Providence of the Father, which was why His healings were always accompanied by prayer rather than by some medical procedure. But whether through science or the healings of Jesus, the intent of the Creator is being brought to fruition in any kind of healing.

We are thankful for the early Christian communities who seem to have recognized the full significance of the healings of Jesus. As they gathered in prayer and remembrance, they must have spent a considerable amount of time reminiscing about their experiences with Jesus, which would certainly have included memories of the healing relief he brought to so many, probably including many of them. They may well have experienced him present with them when they prayed and reminisced on these matters, the same as they experienced him at the Breaking of Bread.

The continuing need for the healing that Jesus brought to so many led them to originate another memorial service. They surely sensed that a healing memorial would be essential if they were to be true to the ministry of Jesus. It may well have taken a while before they realized Jesus meant they were to be healers of others and not just seek their own personal healing as they maybe did while he was physically among them. Their healing ministry would need to be community directed.

The second mistaken notion about sickness is what afflicts us today. Our false notion assumes that our experiences are exclusively body centered. When physical healing takes place, most of us perceive only very limited spiritual connections. While we easily recognize the God-given gift of medical science signifying God's loving care and Providence, there is no appreciation that the Creator's design for Creation has come to fruition through that physical science and healing.

Our experiences of healing at the hands of medical professionals could be greatly enhanced if we did recognize the bigger sphere in which everything takes place. It probably will not advance the healing process itself to know this, but the physical healing experience may well enliven our spirit to a greater extent. Without being able to name it, many of us experience a lingering negative soul effect especially from serious illness, while others are actually energized by healing so that their lives take off with new vigor. This invigoration could be enhanced for everyone were we to recognize the full Creation context of any healing we may experience.

We are creatures who have acquired our material substance from this universe, and consequently our hearts and bodies can never experience totally the fullness of our being if we remain isolated in mind and spirit from earth and universe. Nor will we appreciate fully what is involved in physical healing. In fact, there is more than meets the eye. We are designed by the Creator to be interactive with our universe and we gift ourselves greatly by developing a sense of that wider scope of our human lives. Awareness of this cosmic scope may also advance a more realistic sense of our human capabilities that are quite likely greater than mere physical or intellectual.

We are not speaking here of fancy imaginations like astrology. Some who are into astrology take our cosmic connections to extremes. Trying to mediate cosmic effects by means of crystals and other devices opens many to imagine too much. There may well be a basis in fact for what they are seeking, namely cosmic effects, but their means may not be all that realistic. We do well to let our cosmic connections function as they may without trying to help it along with fanciful additions like crystals. Our best bet is to be open to the Providence of the Creator and not the providence of imagined, unproven avenues to the bounty of the universe.

Sacramental Ministry within the Church deals with more than human needs and Graces, but includes the needs of the earth and the cosmos—all Creation. This may seem preposterous and unreal to many, but both science and Divine Revelation indicate we do not function separate from the universe. Creation is our environment, the source from which we got our physical being. Our souls, the counterpart of our physical bodies, were created to mesh with our physical side and with the physical universe. What we seem to lack is a more unambiguous awareness of our full natural condition.

The historical Jesus of Nazareth took his cosmic connections seriously and even now is present with us as the Cosmic Lord of all Creation. Through him, with him and in him we find our avenue to the healing available to us through Creation. We do not need to invent new connections to the universe or to Creation. We have been created already connected. Jesus of Nazareth recognized in his culturally unscientific way this connection and has established for us a truly human path to the Creator through Creation.

Church Sacraments are more than rites and rituals to keep us occupied in prayerful song and activity. Through the celebration of these Sacraments we walk side by side with the cosmic Christ just as the Apostles did in Gospel days, enjoying the company and being enriched with his own faith and love. In his company we are at the very pinnacle of the Creation process. In his company are to be found the fulfillment of our hopes and dreams for a better life. For sure we will not be free of pain and struggle, but that pain and struggle are concurrent with the progress of Creation toward its goal of fulfillment. Awareness, the goal of Far Eastern spiritual practices can be enriching for anyone, whether from the East, West, North, or South. Genuine awareness of our Creational surroundings will be enlivening, while lack of unawareness leads to stagnation.

We really cannot experience ourselves at our best, traversing the earth unmindful of our Creation connections. There probably are few, if any, who do not sometimes experience some unfathomable sense of incompleteness, possibly a malaise of sorts, a disease. That is probably the original, accumulated effect of sin. Our hearts are not at rest until they rest in God is a well-known, oft repeated truth, but the basic reason for our feeling of distance from God is not so clear. Creation which gave that God connection to even our most ancient ancestors just does not enter the consciousness of most of us, though it is deep within our subconscious. We do know God from the many prayerful connections we have experienced, and that is where we begin. But that connection can be greatly enhanced if we consciously open ourselves to the Creation path. It's natural to us.

21

Marriage Shares in the Potency of the Resurrection of Jesus, though Seemingly Too Idealistic to Most of Us

Jesus was a partygoer. It would seem from the many occasions mentioned in the Gospels he probably never turned down an invitation to dine. But always of equal importance for him was the opportunity to instruct or care for a needy person. A case in point is the time a sinful woman crashed a dinner engagement and positioned herself at the feet of Jesus and dramatically protested her contrition (Lk 7, 36-50). The personal transformation that woman experienced because of how Jesus dealt with her was undoubtedly as profound as her behavior was dramatic.

It was the same when Jesus and his Band of 12 were attending a wedding in Cana of Galilee, perhaps one of many weddings he attended. One of those embarrassing situations everyone probably dreaded developed when the wedding couple learned they had run out of wine—no small matter. From the many extravagant details that John, the Gospel writer, included in the story about how Jesus responded to that problem, it seemed to have been the intention of John the Evangelist to make a needed point of instruction for his contemporary Christian community that may well have been experiencing declining faith and practice.

The Gospel writer John apparently deemed it necessary, eighty or more years after the Resurrection, to remind his community of an important truth about the richness of the new life of Jesus with them. Their life in the New Covenant was much more fruitful than the Old Covenant had been. John very dramatically and deliberately exemplified this by the extravagant amount of wine supposedly provided through the instructions of Jesus in response to the plight of the couple. It was something like the amount of several contemporary fifty-gallon drums, some commentators say. That part of the story was obviously not intended to be taken literally. It was intended to imply that the ministry of Jesus and now the ministry of the Church are copiously more fruitful than the works of the Old Law, John is saying (Jn 2, 1-11).

The Old Law gained its effectiveness from the energetic leadership of Moses, who encountered Yahweh on Mount Sinai amid fire and smoke and thunderous natural commotion. Moses commanded obedience because of his presence at that awesome event that proved his closeness to Yahweh. Jesus, on the other hand, commands the allegiance of the Church because he had been declared beloved of God at the Jordan River at his baptism, and a simple hovering dove was the defining imagery. Nonetheless, at his Resurrection Jesus is enlivened to new life by a Grace greater than Moses experienced on Mount Sinai. God is doing something new and truly marvelous. The Resurrection of Jesus is greater—and therefore the ministry of the Church is greater—is the conclusion John is expressing.

But it is also significant that this instruction was made in the context of a wedding party. There may well have been several layers of instruction in the story, not the least of which might have been that weddings deserve attention in the New Covenant times. Then and now, probably few events in the personal lives of many get as much attention as a wedding. And probably few events in any person's life get as little attention as marriage.

Most people at the time of the Gospel story probably thought Jewish wedding customs were good enough. According to those customs, what really counted was getting the details of wedding ceremony right because everybody knew that what a new married couple really needed is a celebration to establish their place in the community. John the Gospel writer did not seem to intend so much to give an amplifying instruction on marriage as a statement about Jesus the Risen Lord and his meaning for the Church. The Gospel story of John did that masterfully.

But Saint Paul, another Apostle of the teachings of Jesus, also under the inspiration of the Risen Lord Jesus whom he had dramatically encountered in the course of persecuting Christian communities, did write an instruction on marriage. In the course of his teaching, Saint Paul must have often made the point that everything, including marriage, is enriched by the presence of the Resurrected Christ.

After the days and weeks in prayer following his conversion experience, Paul obviously sensed more than anyone else the astounding depth of the teachings of Jesus of Nazareth. It took someone like the highly educated and passionate Paul to catch the difference and proclaim it in speech and writing.

Celibate though Saint Paul may have been, marriage was a matter of no small significance for him. First off, he obviously recognized the profound cultural and religious impact of marriage on individuals and family life. Building on that, he took marriage to heights never before considered. No longer was it to be thought of as just a social convention or a religious ceremony. All that assumed mostly contractual and societal values and human doings, all very customary. In the view of Paul, there was a value to marriage far exceeding anything of human contrivance.

His theologizing about marriage reached its peak in his letter to the Church in Ephesus (Eph, 5, 32-33). Paul begins his instruction explaining how a husband and a wife should treat one another with courtesy and respect, and then astonishingly said: "This is a great mystery. ...*I understand it to mean Christ and his church.*" Marriage, Paul is saying, is a sign of the unity between Christ and his Church. Basing himself on his own experience of the Risen Lord, he seemed to envision the same Grace for everyone Baptized into the Body of Christ. He is suggesting that that Grace can enrich the bond between a man and a woman in marriage.

In that there is a depth of meaning that far exceeds the understanding of any other teaching of the Law. Paul is saying that God gifts couples with an honored place in the Church because a Christian marriage is patterned after Christ's unity with his Church. Christ and the Church share a bond unequaled by any other union in all Creation; and to proclaim that marriage is a sign of that union, that bond, is to give a value to marriage no one before ever taught. This is a renewed understanding of marriage that the risen Lord was able to instill in Saint Paul as he spent those weeks in prayer and reflection after his own experience of the Risen Lord.

So much for then! However, in order for marrying couples in the Church today to appreciate the full meaning of this bond between the Church and the Resurrected Lord, their experience of the Church must be meaningfully and deeply felt. The Church is the principal place to experience the Resurrected Lord, and if the couple has little meaningful experiences either of the Church or of the Resurrected Lord in Sacrament and Liturgy, neither can the bond of Marriage as Paul speaks of it impact their lives.

The Resurrection of the Christ has always been the defining reality of the Church. St. John and St. Paul have suggested that the Christ has put us in touch with that same Creator and Creation. We have an invaluable treasure of earthly, Creation-based Sacraments that mediate the presence of the Resurrected Christ.

Marrying couples need not be able to explain these things, but they do need some down-to-earth experiences of the Creator and the Christ. Then the awesome reality of their marriage bond as St. Paul explained it to the Ephesians can be a source of inspiration and strength. Then the marrying couple as well as the rest of the church will be more surely bonded to the Creator and the Cosmic Christ.

22

A New Passover and a New Covenant
Commissioned to a New Priesthood

Most of us crave moving, soul-stirring experiences that touch us deeply and leave lasting effects. Our Spiritual side can become dried up for lack of such stimuli. There are many sources that can provide this life giving experience: beautiful gardens, enthralling landscapes, the night sky filled with stars, artistic displays, and dramatic presentations. Contrary-wise, certain civil celebrations as well as some religious ones affect us very little, so that one might not even notice the day had come, while others draw us into whole-hearted involvement, like Christmas and the Fourth of July. One's spirits will usually be stimulated with the activities surrounding those days.

That was very definitely true about the Old Covenant celebration of Passover, an event that left its mark on Hebrew society and individuals. Though the original event was long past by Jesus' time, it was still central, maybe better called pivotal to the entire cycle of feasts of the Jewish calendar; and the days of the festival intruded on the lives of almost everyone. It commemorated and resonated with the events that led up to the Exodus from Egypt in the days of Moses. They had been held captive by the Pharaoh of Egypt for some four hundred years when Moses, under the impetus of Yahweh, led the people on a dash to freedom, passing through the Red Sea and wandering through the desert for forty years (cf. Ex, 12, 37-42). That is the stuff of epic stories and movies. Yet the event and subsequent retelling of the story during the annual celebrations of Passover far exceeded any contemporary movie presentation of the event.

Passover was *the* Feast occasioning family and national festivities, full of much pageantry. It celebrated and reinforced the Covenant by keeping alive the memories of Moses, the great lawgiver. Through generations of teachings by many deeply spiritual Rabbis they were constantly reminded of the significance of the Feast. Therefore, for many of the simple as well as educated people, Passover was a powerful and enriching Religious celebration. It could hardly pass without notice and often brought profound Spiritual enrichment to the people.

As an observant Jew and as the Rabbi of his community of Apostles and disciples, Jesus presided as the Celebrant of that Old Covenant Passover Meal the night before he died. Given the situation evolving that threatened the very life of Jesus, and given the profound appreciation of the Feast that characterized the Spirituality of Jesus, that evening in the "upper room" was to be like no other. Those disciples had no idea at the time what was the significance of some of the words and deeds of Jesus that night. Unbeknownst to them, Jesus was presiding as Priest and Victim of a Sacrifice establishing a new and everlasting Covenant; yet there was no way they could get their minds around all that. The Old Sacrifice of a lamb they could understand, but the Seder they shared that night took things beyond their comprehension.

First of all, they did not like the way Jesus was speaking of his own death, even though he seemed to be saying something pretty awesome affecting him and themselves was coming down. It was great that he promised they would be sharing a remembrance cup of wine with him from then on, but that night was full of fear and confusion. They missed the significance of commingling the familiar imagery of sacrificial lamb with references to a new Covenant, and himself as a new sacrificial victim.

There were implications in all this that went beyond Covenant doings they had known, implications that have stirred the soul of all humankind ever after. Jesus the incarnate Word of the Creator, later on will speak words of commissioning to the gathered disciples that will assure the continuance of the ministry of Jesus. It was a ministry bringing healing for the wounds of sin that blemish the image of the Creator stamped on the soul of humankind and all of Creation. The Creator is renewing the face of the earth so all life may find healing. These are events capable of stirring the souls of individuals and nations and whole epochs of Creation time. These are Creation events.

Eventually, after the Resurrection and the opportunity to experience Jesus very much alive with them and to listen to his further teachings, they came to realize the connection between the blood Jesus had shed on the Cross and the blood of the Old Covenant Sacrificial lamb. They eventually realized that the sharing of the cup of wine and loaf of bread in memory of him was to be more than a symbolic memorial as the Old Covenant had been. Jesus said *that* bread was his own body and the wine was his own blood; and so in that sharing of wine and bread Jesus himself would always be present. This was considerably more profound and soul-stirring than the old religious symbols they were accustomed to. What fallible mind could comprehend it? It took the potency of the Resurrection to bring clarity to it all (Mt 26, 26-29).

In due time after the Resurrection, those disciples began to fathom the depth of their calling to be disciples of Jesus. They were to continue the work he had begun no matter how impossible that may have seemed to them. Jesus would formally and most solemnly commission them for the task when he appeared to them in the "upper room" after his Resurrection and said: "As the Father has sent me, so I send you! Go out to all the world." His promise to be with them always began to take on a much deeper significance. Not only would he be a companion as he had been for three years, but his presence as the Risen Lord of this New Covenant would have untold consequences they would only very slowly come to comprehend (Jn 20, 19-23).

There was something in that commissioning by Jesus that went beyond any other handing on of authority they were familiar with. The Resurrected Lord Jesus said to them that just as all authority had been given to him, so he was handing on that authority to them. This is no lightweight matter brought about by ordinary human activity. This is the stuff of Divine magnitude. The Kingdom they were to proclaim was of Divine magnitude. These are not tasks any mere human could even imagine or attempt. Their souls were seared deeply by these experiences as no Old Covenant experiences ever could.

Down through succeeding millennia, building up a structured human institution called the Church will eventually materialize. Out of a treasury of many gifted human persons, bringing along the gifts of art, music, architecture, science, and every form of human endeavor, the Church took root all around the earth. The building of that Kingdom of God Jesus envisioned needed the Grace, the potency of the Risen Lord. It needed more than educated, Spiritually formed Popes, Bishops, and Priests.

It is not the Ecclesial Institution that can bring about that Kingdom, but the abiding presence of the Risen Lord. Even human foibles and evil ways cannot hinder the spreading of the Kingdom of God any more than the reprehensible weaknesses of the Jewish people waiting for Moses to come down from Mount Sinai could not stop their journey to freedom and redemption. The deceit of Judas Iscariot could not stop Jesus from his journey to a new Covenant on the Cross. Even the most devastating human shortcomings present in this Church over the past two millennia cannot deter it from its journey to Redemption. God's purposes for Creation cannot be frustrated.

From within that Institution we call the Church the mechanism to pass on the commissioning the Risen Lord conferred on his Apostles has resided in very simple human matter and form. There are certain gestures, symbols and prayers that have been carried over from the Apostolic times on down to this day in the Sacrament of Orders or Ordination; laying on of hands by an Ordaining Minister; and anointing of candidates with oil for Priesthood and the Episcopacy. The laying on of hands and anointing with oil has a long history of use in Old Testament times. Prophets were anointed and designated by the laying on of hands. Priests of the Old Covenant liturgies were anointed and designated by the laying on of hands. Peter, Paul, and the other Apostles are cited as following this simple gesture when sending out missionaries to far places.

There is something of the timeless, evolving processes of Creation in ageless old customs and practices. It is the Creator's hand hovering over Creation that sustains the ongoing processes commissioned by Jesus. It is the Creator's hand hovering over candidates being anointed for priesthood and episcopacy, bringing to completion Creation and the Kingdom of God. The Resurrection of Jesus from the dead is the ultimate step in the ancient process of Creation and the Kingdom coming to fulfillment. It is the Risen Lord fulfilling his promise to be with his disciples forever, even as long as ongoing Creation.

In the big picture of Creation, Jesus came to realign humankind with Creation's purposes, and to heal the long festering wounds suffered from ages-long, human spirit-destroying greed, injustice, and self-serving enterprises. Their commissioning needed all the potency of Creation itself flowing from the Resurrection. That commissioning was given in the most astounding moment of human history, and was intended to resound down through all succeeding generations of Christian history. They will be Resurrection Churches spreading the fruits of that Kingdom of God. That Church, that sacramental ministry fulfills the plan to make all things new—-a new Creation.

23

Mary, the Mother of Jesus, the Ultimate Exaltation of Creation

There is some likelihood that most of us have not lost our childhood fascination for watching a Fourth of July display of fireworks pompously booming away and extravagantly splashing across the sky above us, while yet waiting for the anticipated finale that we knew would be even better. One might also wonder if perhaps the Creator himself, after the burst of the big bang that sent billions upon billions of stars traveling out into space at unimaginable speed—constantly evolving, forming more complex galactic systems—eventually culminating in one very special planet we call Earth, populated with human life —a planet that eventually would be enriched with a life greater than all previous Creation—a life that arose from the confines of a burial tomb, all of which began with the birth of a child in an animal stable and astonishingly announced by choirs of angels sent forth from the light-filled realm of the Creator. One wonders if the Creator would have felt a spasm of ecstasy when that event planned from the very beginning of these things was coming to fruition. That special but very unspectacular person was named Jesus, born of a mother named Mary. This simple event took place on the face of the earth near a town called Bethlehem, in the Province of Judea in a simple insignificant country under the control of the earthly Roman Empire.

Reflections on that awe-inspiring Creation process would be incomplete without including special attention to this lady, Mother, Queen, and Icon. Without her faith-filled response to the call of an angel, the glorious culmination of the Creator's grand plan for the mind-boggling, eons of time-consuming events and processes of Redemption, could never have come to fulfillment.

The Creator might have said, "I could not have done it without you, Mary!" She accepted her calling to fulfill God's plan in faith and trust without a clear understanding of the angelic presences and words. She had to ponder them in her heart for days and maybe years thereafter. Nevertheless, the Creator's purposes were safely and surely entrusted to her.

In fulfillment of that plan, she gave birth to this son through the intervention of the Holy Spirit and was declared "full of Grace"; full of the grandeur of all Creation, and was proclaimed "blessed among women" (Lk 1, 28). Through her divinely augmented genes, she passed on to her son Jesus the ingredients of a marvelous human being who would be declared by the Father to be his beloved Son. Countless angelic choirs did not congregate to sing at her giving birth for nothing. The Creator had been preparing for this event since time immemorial. It was the "fullness of time" (Eph 1, 10; Gal 4, 4).

The angel-guided role of the mother of Jesus continued on into the fullness of time as disciples of Jesus began to gather in communities called Churches, in fulfillment of the commissioning Jesus gave them to proclaim his good news to the entire world. She continued to fulfill her crucial role by her encouraging and sustaining presence with the Apostles and gathering disciples. It is probably not too much to assume that the Church could not have survived and grown into its commissioned role without the faithful presence of Mary among them. Continuing down the course of two millennia, the Church still experiences her motherly support and encouragement as she appears to selected individuals in particular times of crises.

When she appears, this lady exudes the glory and grandeur of the Court of Heaven to where she had been bodily assumed. She always conveys messages of encouragement and blessings. Nevertheless, some Christians always seem to be looking for a fire-breathing, accusatory zealot type they think we need. If on the other hand, what we are looking for is Mother of Divine Grace, Mother Most Amiable, Mother of our Creator, Mother of our Savior, *that* is whom we will find (Litany of Loretto). The Creator found someone competent to "mother" humankind to a pinnacle of honor and glory, Creation's solitary boast of "fullness of Grace." It is no wonder devotional imagery often places her amidst the stellar realm.

We have spent considerable time in earlier chapters delving into the earliest moments and eons of Creation's beginnings. Much of that was measureless time. Coming to measured time, it matters little how one divides it up, whether a second, hour, day, year, or millennium, it gets our attention. Historic time is often marked off by outstanding persons and events. Mary, the mother of Jesus born into measured time, nonetheless bears the stamp of Creation's timelessness. She has become an icon of serenity, of strength, of steadfast faithfulness to the will of the Creator.

Icon refers to somebody widely admired, symbolizing some movement or field of activity. Truly iconic personalities are few and far between. The cosmic realm however holds more material, nonhuman icons than we can count—the moon, stars, planets, even the earth, all of which have often been revered as icons. The ancients plied their imaginations to picture humanlike personages with extraordinary gifts and roles represented by the stars. There is one special earthly icon who has often been represented with stars around her head and the moon at her feet, not because she is imagined in some special role or accomplishment, but precisely because of who she is.

The cosmic realm of shimmering nighttime stars captures our imaginations and reflections because of how it sprinkles the night sky; and also because of the ever-growing information we have of its vast expanse and uncountable number of items located out there. So too, what the Creator has accomplished, bringing all that created "stuff" to its crowning glory in the person of Jesus of Nazareth, born of Mary, leads to thoughts and imaginations that take on Heavenly proportions. She and her son, even when they walked on the earth among neighbors and acquaintances, were involved in affairs that go beyond earthly matters.

To interact with her in prayer and devotion in time of sickness, pain, or distress of any kind is to avail oneself of potencies flowing from the Kingdom of Heaven. The healing she facilitates is restoration of damaged earthly conditions that curtail full life. Yet we think too small when all we can pray for is healing from some bodily sickness or need. We need the same healings Jesus brought to sufferers, which was seldom just about bodily ailments. The first Christians surely never thought of asking Mary to cure some ailment or provide some earthly need. What they needed and what they were so happy to have was her reassuring presence with them, someone they could talk to, to reminisce with about Jesus and his teachings, someone who could just help make sense of it all.

In the minds and hearts of those first Christians, her personal accounts of angelic experiences and visions must have rung with the echoes of the realm occupied by those angelic choirs, and consequently with resonances from endless space and limitless time. Neither Mary nor anyone at the time could have worked out in their minds the meaning of the birth of her son and his later heartbreaking death on a cross; but eventually the Church came to an understanding that she gave birth to the very creating Word of God who brought the redeeming love of God into the sinful affairs of humankind. Mary's faith-sharing stories must have often left her listeners mystified but fortified in faith and love. These are not matters easily put into logical narration. For several generations, all this was mostly portrayed through the medium of art, poetry, and song.

In later years, often the art has been in the form of medallions. There is probably no medal among the many medals blessed by the Church that is as perennially popular as the Miraculous Medal. We are all familiar with the image of Mary standing on a globe of the earth, with the rays of light streaming towards the earth from her hands, and a serpent or dragon being crushed under her feet. It is an image specifically designed to portray both Heavenly and earthly magnificence.

This image is reminiscent of an image described in the book of Revelations, chapter 12, where a woman and a dragon are described this way: "A great sign appeared in the sky, a woman clothed with the sun, with the moon under her feet, and on her head a crown of twelve stars." It was an image explicitly designed to portray awesome Creator marvels. For the first Christians at the time the Book of Revelations was written, the woman in the vision symbolized God's people in Old Covenant times. This woman, representing the Old Testament Israel, gave birth to the Messiah who then becomes the new Israel, the Church that suffers persecution by a dragon at the time assumed to be the Roman Empire. All this represents the awesome scope of God's history-encompassing work. However, no Marian implications were possible or intended at that time.

Over time, as the mother of Jesus gained prominence in the minds and hearts of the long- suffering Christian communities, it was recognized that the image of the woman threatened by the dragon could also refer to Mary the mother of Jesus threatened by the serpent representing worldwide evil. Both the Old Testament and the New Testament images are epochal in significance, keeping before the eyes of believers the Creator's grand work of ongoing Salvation, as well as the place of Mary in that work. So much Divine activity is depicted on such a small article as this Miraculous Medal!

In the same way, prayer and devotion to Mary even today can be and needs to be invigorated with that same Creation-inspired dynamism. Our problem seems to be we lack that Creation-centered insight that guided the Spirituality of Mary and Jesus. Our prayer requests need to be released from the less important individual needs, to soar to the realm of worldwide magnitudes. Only then will we experience the genuine enrichment the first century Christians obviously knew so well stemming from their relationship to Mary.

We need not be timid to expect much from God and from Mary, though it may not be what we think it should be. What the Creator has in store for us may even be beyond what we can imagine. God thinks and acts big, as big as all Creation. True devotion to Mary will lead in just that direction, though without seeking exciting miracles that can only satisfy temporary fancy. This mother, this fellow disciple has been an abiding presence in all circumstances of the Church ever since.

This quite likely came about because of the words Jesus spoke to the Disciple John from the Cross: "This is your mother," and to Mary, "This is your son" (Jn 19, 26). At that very moment, Jesus was on the threshold of his Kingdom where he now reigns as Lord of all Creation, so those words carried immense weightiness. The early Church eventually learned that those words would have heartening consequences for their benefit and to the honor of Mary. Quite likely, Mary herself would have reminded John and the gathering Christians of those words and other teachings that were typical of Jesus.

She might well have helped them call to mind an earlier occasion when she and some of his cousins were standing outside where Jesus is teaching and requested that he come out to them. His somewhat puzzling reply to that request carries connotations beyond the moment. His response to an ordinary family concern for his well-being has led to some extraordinary consequences for those of us who consider ourselves his disciples. Most surprisingly, he said anyone who hears the Word of God and acts on it is mother, brother, and sister to him—*they are family to him* (Mk 31-35; Mt 12, 46-50; Lk 8, 19-21).

Jesus was not into meaningless, offhand statements. The implication is that he really intended to extend his family to include every disciple doing the will of God, even on down to us today. It is a privilege to be cherished and celebrated. Many seem to miss the marvel of the special gift of family being offered because the first thought is the assumption of a responsibility to do something—do the will of the Father. Implied obligations, yes; nonetheless those words *at the time* quite likely added to a growing sense of a family relationship among the disciples. They knew Jesus always meant what he said, and besides, they needed this family association.

Mary has been Assumed (bodily taken) into Heaven so that wherever we go or whatever we do, she will have been there before us with stars around her head and the moon at her feet. Hold that image! There is power and even glory resonating from that image. Thankfully, the responses of Mary are more than equal to the needs of our petitions. No matter the meagerness of our prayers, her responses are bountiful. She is mother of the very Word of the Creator, the Word that made every good gift of Creation. We pray in order to open ourselves to that Word. That Word has made us part of her extended family, so we are brothers and sisters of that Word.

By prayer, we position ourselves, along with Mary herself, at the wellsprings of Creations' own bounty. We are invited to pray that expansively.

Nothing less can calm our fears that all too often cause a paralysis of hope and love and of aspirations. There are many who easily fall victim to the conviction that nothing really can get better, and thus ends any hope of full life! This may be so because we think and pray about things too small for our own good or the good of those for whom we are praying. That is why it is good to follow the oft repeated advice to leave all matters in the hands of God or perhaps in the hands of Mary.

What Mary always contributes is the presence of a person of uncommon faith, hope, and love. Her persona shaped by her role as mother and disciple of the Son of Man, present at the terrible Crucifixion and at the scene of the Resurrection, then present at Pentecost, earned for her title after title: Mirror of Justice; Seat of Wisdom, Spiritual Vessel, Vessel of Honor, Mystical Rose, Tower of David, Tower of Ivory, Ark of the Covenant, Gate of Heaven, Morning Star, Queen of Angels, of Patriarchs, Prophets, Apostles, Martyrs, Queen of Peace—to name just a few (Litany of Loretto).

Tucked away in that Litany is the invocation: Mother of Good Counsel, pray for us. I think it can be assumed that *good counsel* must have been one of her most sought-after mentoring assets. The Seat of Wisdom invocation refines that image exquisitely; and Morning Star gives her the preeminence that only the cosmos can confer. We are invited to rise up from attention to our less significant needs to nothing less than the processes of Creation itself.

24

Stars and Christmas Travelers

Other than Mary, Joseph, and the child Jesus, there is probably no other feature in the Christmas narrative more distinctive than the star. Singing angel choirs are also depicted in many stylistic ways, but angels are otherworldly while the star is this world. We would do well to ignore all the speculation about the scientific explanation for that mysterious star because any star out there could have been the one.

That star grabs our thoughts and sentiments not only because it is part of the Christmas scene, but also because it shines with cosmic light and creational radiance. Without need to reason it out, our whole being instinctively senses our connection to that star. Our physical makeup of matter brought together from all over the universe during the processes of the evolving universe leads us to instinctively sense a connection to any physical object, be it just a rock from the surface of the earth, or an enormous object like a star. Moreover, when the star is associated with a special Divine intervention in earthly human affairs, it becomes especially stirring to the human spirit.

That star the Magi followed is real even though science may never be able to pinpoint just which of the myriads of stars out there was the one that caught the attention of those mystic-minded astrologers. However it makes *creation sense* that the Creator would choose some item of the universe like a star to announce that Creation was approaching a pinnacle of majesty and glory. Previous cultures and peoples sought and found the Creator through their observations of that universe as displayed in the night sky, so there is little wonder that the Creator would inspire these three men of faith to understand that a special personage was about to appear on the scene of human history, and reveal this through the medium of one of the stars that had possibly been burning its light since earliest time!

Science tells us those stars are actually traveling further away from one another out into space all the time, so the *traveling* star as depicted in the Christmas story even scientifically fits the Biblical narration. But those mystic minded scientists would be attracted to that star not scientifically but in faith. It seems clear that well before our era of science, humankind was attuned to greater realities of the universe than our contemporary sciences can ever detect. They were in touch with *Creation's* Creator.

It may be that we lose something very important in our Nativity celebration when those three Wise Men and their majestic camels do not show up Liturgically until the feast of Epiphany two weeks later. They have become more like an afterthought because by then we are winding down from the main focus—the birthday of Jesus of Nazareth, and so our attention to the Wise Men loses much of its effectiveness. That is unfortunate because they bring a cosmic/Creational perspective to the Christmas event which really merits more consideration than is allotted.

The manifestation of the Nativity of Jesus to the world depended on a star, and those Magi from the world at large recognized the Divine event because they were open in faith to the self-revelations of the Creator. There was really a remarkable concurrence of all Creation taking place that fills out the Nativity event—the human component, the earthly and cosmic components, and the angelic representing the realm of the Divine. A truly wondrous stage is set fit for a Creationwide presentation.

The tremendous work of creating this universe did not come to a conclusion with the creation of humankind, but was about to find its fulfillment in the coming of one of humankind's own, the birth of a child born into Creation by a human mother. All of the universe represented by that star is involved in this grand enterprise, and humankind is privileged to be at the very center of it all.

Nothing less than this can explain how Christmas has remained such a captivating celebration almost everywhere across the face of the earth. Even though contemporary irreligious secularity is having substantial negative effects on individual and community responses to Christmas, the attraction of this grand Creation event can never be erased from the mind and heart of humankind. We are not only celebrating a Church festival, we are celebrating a Creation event. The combined cosmic attendances and faith sensitivities are powerful pulls on the human heart. The Creator would likely win any tug-of-war contest over this.

Whether they recognize it or not, when any people, nation, or culture, celebrates noteworthy persons or events of their history, they are celebrating Creation history. The same thing is true of living individuals who celebrate birthdays or anniversaries; they too are events taking place in Creation history. The birth of the Messiah into that earthly and cosmic association makes it powerfully vibrant and celebratory. The entrance of those Magi on the scene adds an earthly and cosmic/creational dynamism to the event and to our celebrations. Were we to pay attention, all those combined concurrences can play a commanding role in vitalizing Christmas celebrations everywhere.

The journey of those Magi and the worldwide journey of humankind are not finished because Creation itself is not finished. We have miles and eons to go and we need the faith and tenacity of those Magi for the journey. Their strong faith sensitivities gave them the confidence God was preparing something important in the course of human and earthly history and they wanted to be there in order to be blessed by the event.

One can wonder what might have been their thoughts and conversations as they traveled on this auspicious journey. What set them on this journey in the first place came from observing the awesome universe in the night sky, and their hearts must have throbbed with wonder and expectancy every time they looked skyward. All the power of the universe that had set them on their journey must have enveloped them in some kind of star like burn.

And when they came upon the simple scene in a stable of animals, how their minds and hearts must have raced in wonder to find a reason for this turn of the events! Scripture indicates they were secure in their faith and in their "science" of the mysterious universe and went home quite likely satisfied they had found the one for whom they were searching. There are many legends about them and especially their lives after this journey, but we can let it be as it is described in the Gospel (Mt 2, 1-12).

But we cannot let it go without asking ourselves some important questions about what we see or discern when we look up at the sky. Unfortunately we probably only notice if it is a sunny or a cloudy day and wonder if it is going to rain or snow on our event. We can look at the stars at night and observe they are nice to look at, and science programs on TV give a lot of facts and pictures that are interesting, but it is all so far away and doesn't seem to affect us much. We miss so much of the full impact of the event if all we hope to do is "have a Merry Christmas." Something earth shattering took place there that we desperately need to incorporate into our celebrations.

There are a lot of things happening on the face of the earth that affect the lives of every one of us. Most people are aware of the news about earth-shaking, human life disrupting situations coming from everywhere across the globe, threatening so much of humankind's life-sustaining necessities. Earth, soil and air contamination, reckless depletion of natural resources, and life-threatening climate changes stemming from human causes are constants in the news. And more than quality of life is in the balance.

Some of us do become concerned but there seems to be nothing that prompts the same kind of action the Magi took when they went seeking solutions to their problems, which were likely substantial. Their wisdom led them to seek recourse beyond the usual sources no matter the cost in travel and personal assets so they brought along substantial gifts. Those gifts, no matter what they actually were, represented their deep-down commitment to what might be incumbent on them in follow-up to their search and travels. Knowing what we do from our contemporary political experiences, those Magi quite likely had to maneuver around persistent calls to solutions less demanding of established order and personal assets than they might have suggested. They were not called "Wise Men" for nothing because they were aiming at real solutions embodied in a Divine message known from the stars.

And here we are today facing situations almost for sure more dire than those Magi were facing. Even without seeking Divine answers, our sciences give us very clear data about our situation. Those sciences of course are themselves Divine gifts which we dare not ignore. The Creator is speaking through those sciences in compelling ways and yet we do not have to get on our camels to find the resources we need. Our solutions are at hand but we seem to lack the vigor to act. If we are seeking patron saints for our times and situation, those Magi suit the bill.

From their place now in the realm of eternity, they might be prodding us to look to the sky where they and countless forbearers found the necessary Divine invigoration for crucial actions. If the cave dwellers or whoever were our forbearers could navigate the complexities of their times and venture out to make better homes for themselves, what is holding us back? Why do we stand looking vacant-minded up to the sky only looking for pleasantries, when our earthly home is hovering at a cliff's edge?

We recycle a few things we want to get out of our way, industrialists are constantly devising technologies and fabrications truly remarkable and constructive, but we continue making little headway toward the deep-down, earth wide basics of our earthly problems. We have not gotten serious about how much we really care about the earth. We need take the Magi journey.

But that will entail more than saddling the camels. What are going to be the gifts we take along? To what are we committing ourselves? What star are we following? Is it a twinkling trinket or a raging fiery star like our sun? This journey is going to need the energy of suns, and that is not just poetic imagery. We may not believe it but we do function in that cosmic league; and while most of the stars are farther away than we can even measure, their energy has played a role in our very material formation. The Creator made it to be so for our benefit, but if we do not draw from that Creationwide source of Divine Providence, we will not be equal to the task ahead of us. The Magi were able to do it, but we seem to not take their journey seriously. We seem to believe it is nothing more than a quaint story. However we do need make that Magi journey! How many more Christmases must we celebrate before we saddle the camels and get on our way?

25

Creation Deserves Better

We have lived too long mindful only of necessary gainful enterprises and the physical benefits provided from the material bounty of the earth, but unmindful that the Creator has designed it all to promote human life on this earth in ways much more profound than all that. When I plant a garden, I probably experience myself doing very fulfilling work out in nature, but that gardening does more than provide produce for table and pleasing displays. Were I mindful of it, my soul could be stimulated even more deeply than nature alone can do. I am involved in more than earthly agronomy, as full of little biological miracles as that is. I am involved in the phenomenal, universe wide miracles of ongoing Divine creation. I am enormously more productive than I can imagine.

Any productive human activity partakes in the creativity of the Creator. The question then is not how do I get off the earth and into all that creativity, but how I *align myself in mind and soul* with all that continuing Divine Creation taking place through my earthly instrumentality. It is no small thing to plant and tend to a garden, to make something new grow on the face of this garden planet earth.

The mineral ingredients of the soil at one time existed in different forms far out in space before being gathered together to form this planet. Any kind of garden or even a houseplant literally brings the entire physical universe together in a little earthly creation. I do not need science or any kind of intellectual acumen to do that. Everything that I plan or do partakes in the reality, the grandeur, the astounding wonder of God's own Creation. No small thing! Am I looking for something of importance to do to find fulfillment. There it is!

Knowing all this may not make that garden or houseplant grow any better, but it will help me see into the awesome interconnections of which I am a part. I was designed to mesh in mind and body with this physical universe though I do not make that happen no matter my intellectual or educational attainments. This is all Creator originality. This is astounding reality beyond the sphere of any science yet was not unknown to even earliest people on the earth. The human soul subconsciously experiences these realities of the universe and longs for opportunities for productive work.

Humankind is fundamentally integral to the Creation process and is exquisitely equipped to give expression to creativity in multitudes of settings, times, and situations. Unfortunately, once the many scientific enterprises began accumulating, we became distracted from reverencing the Creator who gifted humankind with our superlative gifts, and became unmindful of our Divine instruction to tend the earth as a garden. Nonetheless, it will not serve the mission of faith to belittle or put down science. The advantages of science-enhanced enterprises and products are too many and even too indispensable to be denied. For persons of faith, all these advances in creativity do not destroy faith but call forth thanksgiving for these expressions of beauty and utility.

It is deplorable that humans have devised destructive uses never intended by the Creator, making the healing potential of Creation so valuable and even necessary. We cannot go on putting so much effort into devising medicinal remedies needed because of our carelessness or evil intents. Not only better medical science is needed, but a more explicit grounding in a Creation conscience. Most folks quite likely recognize the promptings of an inner voice called conscience, but beyond that *conscious* conscience, a basic *Creation-formed* conscience is active in the human person even before we begin intellectual or volitional activity to form a conscience. That deep-down voice of conscience is the original creational tendency toward the common good of all Creation including the good of humankind. That good includes beneficial human interaction with the earth

The Biblical Genesis story of Creation described how the Creator inspired a conscious conscience in humankind to care for the earth garden. The story includes how Adam and Eve (humankind) succumbed to a temptation to disregard the good of the garden for the sake of personal gratification and ruined (lost) the garden. It is not difficult to recognize the ongoing sin and the harmful effects accumulating to the detriment of human life and to the earth garden.

The basic intent of this book has been to gather all things under the umbrella of Creation from which we gain the sense of our Creator grounding. We could gain powerful personal and communal vitality from recognizing that we are always functioning within active Creation through which we are gifted with Divine Providence. This Providence fosters a drive for genuine progress to a better life. This Providence ensures us that the Creator truly wants us to progress to better things.

The morally correct way to live on this earth is to contribute to its physical growth to fullness of being. Mountains are constantly growing, valleys, and canyons are always changing, rivers are constantly changing course, and even oceans keep changing coastlines and bottom contours. All of that is actually constructive to the earth because it is creating new beauty, grandeur, and variety. It is part of ongoing creation.

Many large industrial enterprises also require massive earthmoving, digging into the earth, rearranging the surface of the earth. In some small sense all that is the same as Creation's processes, but often there is a big difference. Industrial earthmoving is not done to improve the earth but to satisfy the desire for profitable gain, and the outcome for the earth will not always be beneficial. Often unhealthy debris is left over that improves neither the earth nor human life.

Our understanding of true progress can be perceived in the depth of our soul if we follow the innate inclination of our Creation conscience. These are things not easily perceived by everyone, so instructions by enlightened Spiritual guides are always needed. In Old Testament times it was mainly the Prophets whom God enlightened for this purpose. Those holy Prophets and others, including songwriters, have left a treasure trove of soul-stirring and instructive literature. Among such treasures is Psalm 104, which is reproduced in the appendix of this book. That Psalm has been a valuable source of insights into the wonder of Creation for Jews and Gentiles down through these many generations.

In due time, Jesus of Nazareth came among us and left a trove of teachings in the New Testament Gospels. He very solemnly commissioned his disciples to gather in communities wherein he could be present and continue his ministry of teaching and healing the wounds of sin, wounds that are accumulating in ever-increasing magnitude. The earth and humankind deserve and desperately need this ministry, and the churches are endowed with the Spirit of the Cosmic Christ that can lead us on into an enlightened view of that future.

26

Everything is Creation, Not Excluding the Church

It is doubtful a supercomputer exists capable of calculating the accurate numbers, magnitudes, distances, and whatnot all involved in measuring the universe. Quite likely, there have been individuals down through history who have tried to count the stars visible in the night sky, though no doubt that too was found to be an impossible task. In addition to these huge items anyone can see in the sky, everything else one can think of on the face of the earth, including persons and human institutions, all have special significance in reference to Creation.

Unfortunately, the only recognized value they possess depends on some immediate usefulness. Does it provide good economic and political gain or enjoyable satisfaction? Nothing I will be saying hereafter devalues those pragmatic needs because human life cannot be of good quality without those many functional associations, or without the production of the goods everyone relies on. However, there is the more basic value that underlies all that, namely Creation itself.

One such human association never evaluated in reference to Creation is the Church, and this to the detriment of both the Church and ourselves. As a consequence, an attitude seems to have developed within many of the Churches that the physical wellbeing of the earth is of little pertinence to the commitments of the church. For too long only a passing notice was given to care for the earth, if it was recognized at all. The truth seems to have been lost that in the Genesis story of Creation instructions were given to Adam and Eve to care for the garden they inhabited. Little thought seems to have been given to the fact that they lost their paradise due to selfish concerns that suited their

111

tastes rather than the concerns of the garden (cf. Gen 3, 1-7, *Second Story of Creation—The Fall*). Eating the forbidden fruit as the serpent led them to do represented disobedience to the command to care for the garden and not just satisfy their own desires. Truth to be told now, are we doing any better with the garden today? Quite likely not, yet most churches let that pass with little attention to the Scriptural-based moral question involved.

Everything that the physical care and utilization of the earth calls us to—that is where Church ministry calls us. Until that full sense of the role of the Church is appreciated, the official defined responsibilities of membership in the Churches are going to be inadequate for the Spiritual needs of their membership. Scientific advances to cope with changing human needs are going on all the time, but without moral and faith guidelines, scientific and cultural values go astray.

Unfortunately, one reason why Churches have not always risen to the challenges very well, is because of an inadequate sense of *good conduct*. Good conduct has not included a moral stance on our obligations to the earth and its environs. In order for Church ministry to be a positive catalyst within social, political, and economic affairs, it must recognize its own grounding in Creation. The church is the spokesperson of the Divine who is known primarily from Creation. But if the church ignores its grounding in physical Creation as though it functions on a higher level, it will lose its effectiveness and standing among worldwide institutions and appear to be irrelevant to everyday affairs of its members.

Jesus taught and ministered effectively by means of all things earthly. He was respected for that. He was not a miracle worker functioning somehow above the physical state of affairs. He did not need to perform miracles, though the miraculous often enough followed from his presence and words. However, if we today become too absorbed in looking for signs of the miraculous to improve human conditions, we quite likely will miss the full potential of natural Creation, and more importantly may misdirect Church ministries.

Even though it could not have been part of the attention of Jesus, a vital ministry of the Church today will be to teach that it is a moral imperative that enterprises cannot go on functioning as though they are separate from the needs of the earth. Science already recognizes that the laws of nature generally tend toward the good of nature, yet science alone will not be able to deter these harmful tendencies. Faith on the other hand touches the human Spirit more powerfully than ordinary knowledge because faith is directly inspired by the Creator. Through the powerful impetus of the Holy Spirit of the Creator, the Church can provide the motivating drive needed for a change in the harmful trajectory of human enterprises.

Fortunately, no one Church stands alone in this calling. Each and every Christian and non-Christian faith community shares the same potency of faith, the same responsibility. There is evidence that these multicultural faith communities are effectively promoting some important changes in thinking and practice, though still inadequately. We are facing tribulations that outweigh any of the difficulties the Church needed to deal with at any time in its history. It is not just a nation, a culture or any single area of the earth standing in the breach of possible disaster. It is the earth itself and all life forms within its confines.

Unfortunately, a pervasive and aggressive irreligious secularity is having its effect, and Religion is gaining an ever-more negative reputation. Science certainly cannot reestablish Religion, nor take the blame for this situation. Effectual faith practice needs the communal assistance of a Church. "But if salt has lost its flavor, of what use is it?" (Mt 5, 13). Perhaps because the Churches have given the impression they function to provide instructions for the way out of this wicked world in order to gain Heaven, they are perceived as irrelevant as far as worldly affairs are concerned. Too many believe Churches are only concerned with what is wrong with the world and cannot be trusted in anything constructive it says about worldly affairs.

The Church cannot function as though it is not at home in this world. When Jesus prayed that his followers be saved from "this world," he meant to be saved from the evils of the times and not from the world itself. Jesus knew the world itself is not evil, but humankind has sown the seeds of evil. Jesus saw his ministry as a healer of the wounds of sin that trouble everyone, not as a judge of sinners. He was not intent on anything that would inflict a similar kind of violence that sin brought into the world.

In one of his parables he tells the story of a land owner who discovered his fields were infected with excessive weeds. He realized an enemy had sown the weeds (Mt 13, 24-30). But contrary to the wishes of his servants who wanted to pull out the weeds, they were advised not to do so because that would destroy the entire crop. The implication for his disciple was that they were not to follow the teaching of the Scribes and Pharisees who promoted in effect the violence of pulling out the weeds from among the people. What they were doing with their supposed reforms was even more harmful than the evil they wanted to eradicate. Obviously the parable has implications for today or any time.

It is imperative that the church not lose sight of the earthly details of the parables of Jesus because there was a natural potency in those stories that invigorated his listeners and potentially can do the same today. The Grace of the Creator built upon the natural foundation of these stories and empowered disciples to genuine renewal. Those stories can do the same for us today even though we live more detached from agricultural matters. Actually, one does not need to be a farmer to be affected by that Grace. Any scientific explanation of biology learned in school will suffice.

Because we seem to have missed the meaning and Grace of that story, the Church has always proceeded as though its duty is to be tough and eradicate the evil of sin and never mind the off-putting pain that might be inflicted. We may not be using the brutal means of the Inquisition, but for too many it is construed as a sign of weakness and compromising with evil if the Church eases up on certain penalties for noncompliance with Ecclesial directives. That supposed necessity to be hard on sin may well have trumped the command of universal love and mercy even for enemies.

Over time, humankind has picked up on that and follows through with the use of the brutality of war to eradicate the evil of our enemies. We seem not to be able to resist the urge to pull up the weeds. Jesus knew that full well, which may have been why he told that parable. It seems imperative in order to regain its place in the estimation of our culture that the Church must regain the sense of its earthiness as Jesus himself and the disciples of Jesus knew themselves. Only then will the natural potency of his parables penetrate our being. We all too easily gloss over that earthly grounding and try to fly where our church wings cannot carry us.

The Word of God proclaimed in and out of Church is what gives the Churches their power and effectiveness. The Word of the Creator and of Jesus his Son is vibrant in Scripture and Sacramental practices. That Divine Word is speaking the words of a new Creation, and we are that new Creation. Our own words now echo the Words of the Son of God who came completely in step with Creation. His birth, life, teachings, and ministries all complemented Creation.

In the Book of Revelations, the final book of the New Testament, John the Evangelist describes a vision he had concerning the future of the Church. This vision probably came at a time when Christian Churches were experiencing difficult times and flagging faith. In light of the vision, John gives assurance to the Christian community that the Creator still has great things in mind for them.

For John the Gospel writer, this New Creation will not be separate from the former but will be a fulfillment of the old. "Then I saw a new heaven and a new earth. ...I heard a loud voice from the throne cry out: This is God's dwelling among men. He shall dwell with them and they shall be his people and he shall be their God who is always with them. ...The One who sat on the throne said to me, See, I am making all things new!" (Rev 21, 1-5). The Creator promises to live with his people, making them a New Creation, and consequently does not destroy the old but enlivens his people with new life.

We can be assured by this that our own state of crisis today is actually a stepping stone to a better future, not a sign of the end. Nonetheless, if we remain unmindful of this vision the Creator has in mind for us, we doom ourselves to continue on a slippery slope that can only get worse. We might be tempted to ignore that vision of St John as though it were illusory, unrealistic. Nonetheless, if we do not pay attention to those words of promise we will never become the Church envisioned by St John. Jesus himself gave hints of possibilities for the church when he said: If we remain in him, all things are possible. We should know Jesus never thought of or intended small possibilities.

Enlightened by this line of thinking and these teachings, we might actually project a more favorable and inviting image of ourselves. We then might not be afraid of more down to earth images of the Church, rather than images of perfection that intimidate. Our God accepts us as we are because we are loveable, not because we are perfect. It is our sinful but loveable selves that the Creator transforms into a New Creation. Yet, our New Creation image should not show up as some kind of Pharisaical superior image. Our promised New Creation status builds upon our humble earthly selves.

When Jesus spoke to his very human disciples intending to give them courage and conviction, he used the image of leaven in baking dough, which in the hands of a baker and through the action of yeast rises to greater volume; and after baking in an oven becomes a whole new creation, rich in flavor, nourishment, and life giving possibilities. Now, there are some images worth claiming as our own. There are few people who do not enjoy feasting on bread. Perhaps it would help if the Church consistently envisioned and spoke of itself in that flavorful way. Then it might become more appealing to those in need of Spiritual nourishment, or perhaps in need of the celebratory effects of bread. After all, the Church is always celebrating something, though *obligated routine* celebrations lose something of the experience of a celebration. If Liturgy and Sacrament are not experienced as celebrations, all the theological explanations will mean nothing.

Any sort of image that flows from earthly or cosmic foundations is Creation grounded, whether we consciously think of that or not. Our whole being naturally resonates with earthly and cosmic realities because they and we are creational. Culturally and Covenant-wise Jesus was naturally and Spiritually Creation aware, whereas our culture is nature aware. But to gain the full value of being nature grounded we do well consciously to think Creation. It is probably a matter of training ourselves in this way of thinking. However that will never come about if the teaching Church itself does not get on that track. Creation has been too much of an abstraction, or at best a second thought.

There are many in the Churches who lament the diminishing impact of religion and faith on culture and human affair as though that spelt the demise of the Church. On the contrary, as the Psalmist says, we are being "tested and refined like gold in a fiery furnace" (Ps 66, 10), which is imagery that makes reference to the tremendous fiery processes of Creation itself. That imagery is a good fit because the Church is always in a process of change along with the world to which it seeks to minister. Both changes are colossal in scope—they are creational.

When we think of the Church in its weakened, sinful human components, it will always be seen as vulnerable and susceptible to possible demise. We need keep in mind all the Spirit-filled happenings that have emblazoned its history because the Spirit of the Risen Lord has been active especially during all the bad times. Through its Sacred Scriptures it is the earthly sounding board of the Word of the Creator. The very potency of ongoing Creation is at work within; as is the awesome light of new Resurrection life; along with echoes of the blasting winds and blazing fires of Pentecost; and the Words of earth wide and cosmos-encompassing commissioning by the Risen Lord for the Redeeming Works of the Spirit of Jesus the Christ.

Creator, Son, and Holy Spirit each find within the Church their preferred dwelling place and throne from which to reign over all Creation—no small distinction. From within the Church the wounds of sin that wrought disorder and suffering all across the face of the earth find their redeeming healing. From here, the human stewards of Creation begin their work. From here, a New Creation comes into being. The Church really is not just another social institution competing for worldly recognition, nor the institution so many today say they do not trust.

But first the members of the Church themselves need to be attentive to these glories that are celebrated in Liturgy and Sacrament. We need let the earthly and creational wonders that are incorporated in Liturgy and Sacrament sear our senses. For this to happen, the church needs to settle into its earthly, creational level where the splendor of the realm of the Creator is imprinted on every little bit and piece of Creation.

Part of the glory of the Church is that it is leaven in the dough of Creation rising to greater fullness all the time. It is gifted with the ingredients for nourishment and tasteful satisfaction of the human Spirit. But if the Church is not experienced as an agreeable nourishing place to be, then Creator, Son, and Spirit get a tarnished name. They do, after all, claim proprietorial rights in the Church—it is their domain. We honor the Creator when we honor Creation as it is celebrated within Church Rites.

In our culture, brand names have become more important than the product itself. Even a good product without a good brand reputation probably will not do well in the current environment. To be recognized as a vital human institution in this culture, the Church must establish its brand name not based on the stature and prestige of Popes, Bishops, Priests and Ministers of varying sorts, nor on the dignity and splendor of its rites, nor on its history of promoting the arts and sciences, but it must be recognized as following in the foot-steps of Jesus of the Gospels who was thoroughly earth and cosmos oriented. This Church will value everyone as the Creator values all of Creation. Its members must be all that inclusive in the ministries taken on in the name of Jesus.

Our contemporary brand will need to include an even broader sharing of resources than the early church practiced. It must be particularized to include caring enough for one another that we curb the industrial enterprises that do untold damage that affects the well-being of everyone. That is how we must love one another today, and if this is not done out of a motive of Creationwide love, it will gradually diminish to the same old, same old.

The effectiveness of the Church will be judged not only on its opposition to commonly recognized immorality (hot button issues), but on its opposition to prevalent evils that many may not even recognize due to cultural predispositions, especially evil done to the earth. This church will be of assistance to those who seek ways to get beyond their declining cultural ways to new and revitalized values. To do this, it must recognize those disruptive values.

It is time the Churches decide to take unequivocal stance on what is the moral issue of the times. Pope Francis has chided the Church for being too preoccupied with certain moral issues which certainly do need to be dealt with but which are keeping the Church from more compelling issues that have vital life and death effects on each and every person who walks upon the face of the earth. Finely, we need to be prepared to go on into a future for the Church that may not be of our choosing. Actually the Church has always said it goes where the Holy Spirit leads us, and we need expect some grand surprises.

27

Extraterrestrials: The Complete Creation Ecosystem

So far in this book I have considered Creation to be synonymous with the universe as we have come to know it. However, that probably is not an accurate estimation of the extent of the physical universe. Sages of ancient cultures as well as scientists, philosophers, and theologians of almost every period of human history have given thought to the matter of possible extraterrestrial life forms scattered throughout the universe. Some ancients and even first century Christian thinkers imagined that the stars visible in the night sky were living beings with some kind of soul. Absent our contemporary science, it would not be too hard to imagine this to be so.

But even beyond the visible stars, it was assumed the universe was filled with living creatures who were more like angels. In short, the earth was not thought of as standing alone in the universe possessing life. (Cf. a book titled *Vast Universe* by Thomas F. O'Meara, published by Liturgical Press of Collegeville MN, 2012. Its subtitle, *Extraterrestrials and Christian Revelation*, says what the book is about. Michael J. Crowe, also of Notre Dame University, has also authored books on extraterrestrials.)

According these authors, Aristotle and Plato of Greek philosophical fame both had reflected on the *logical* possibilities of "other worlds." While most of these earlier scientists and theologians did not envision much if any interaction with extraterrestrials, the consideration of logical *possibilities* opened the door to what inevitably followed as scientific knowledge of the cosmos expanded. No sooner did telescopes begin opening up new vistas of the universe than evidence began to accumulate that there was much more than meets the eye out there. The one abiding scientific and philosophical question has always been: why is there so much stuff out in the universe?

Professor O'Meara and Michael Crowe have spelled out in some detail the history of evolving thought and publications on the topic. While the supporting science has been very sketchy, the subject has never been out of mind and imagination; and theological implications were also constantly being discussed. O'Meara listed many philosophers, theologians, and authors who have taught and written on the topic, including Origin, a second-century writer; thirteenth-century Saint Thomas Aquinas; the more current nineteenth-century Pierre Teilhard de Chardin; and somewhat earlier Protestants like Melanchthon, Ralph Waldo Emerson, Ellen White, and Paul Tillich, to name just a few. However, it was generally agreed that Sacred Scripture has revealed nothing on the question.

As the complexity of the observable universe becomes more evident through advances in astronomy and discoveries in micro composition of matter continue progressing, the theoretical possibilities of different life forms in far-off galaxies are becoming more and more likely—and for many scientists, it is almost certain. As they become more aware of the mass of the universe and the distances between different galaxies, and observe the existence of gases and matter shooting out from evolving supernova (exploding stars) indicating the probable formation of a new cosmic structures, scientific assumptions about possible "new worlds" have become more precise. Not satisfied with speculations and theories, vastly improved telescopes and large groupings of telescopes have been searching for signs of other planets that could support life forms, as we know life; and other instruments have been tuned in for possible signals from stellar civilizations. The interest and powerful instruments keep evolving, hopefully to bring some closure to this endless speculation. It is the nature of humankind to seek and find answers to the mysteries of the universe.

The fruit of all this effort is that stars and galaxies have actually been observed coming into existence as supernovas break up and seemingly re-form into new structures. It is assumed that individual stars and entire galaxies have continuously *come and gone* over eons measured in billions and even trillions of years. Further, it is assumed that much of this activity is so far away from us that the light from many of them has not yet reached us, and in fact may never reach us even traveling at the assumed speed exceeding 186 million miles a second. All this makes it impossible to observe much of what is going on "out there." Consequently, we may never know what stars and galaxies have gone out of existence over the course of billions of years, and what may still be coming into existence. Curiosity to know and scientific efforts to understand will remain alive and active, and probably productive of many more astounding discoveries.

Among all the differing life forms that might exist, there may well be communities of beings that function not only on a single planet like the earth, but actually exist and function on galaxywide scales. (Wouldn't it be great to vacation throughout the Milky Way?) All of this presupposes material realities that function in ways entirely different from our own. Therefore, not only would that materiality be different, but even Spiritual functions would not be like our own. Their way of knowing, willing and communicating, along with travel and occupations would be vastly different. For the time being, such differences cannot be factually described but can only be imagined. One thing is sure though, Divine ingenuity is limitless.

We have always assumed humankind was the peak of created reality, but that may not be true. We may be amoeba like in capabilities compared to what the Creator may have made in far distant areas of the universe. Whatever actually does exist somewhere in Creation, the Creator would certainly have revealed himself to these other cosmic beings in ways that are particular to them, including perhaps possible interventions of Divine Incarnation? Redemption from sin? Spiritual restorative activities? At this point in time and stage of theological reflections, all this can only be interesting speculations.

There is certainly much gain for us to reflect on our cultural reactions to the possibilities of other life forms. It is sad that popular speculation so often presupposes that aliens will be dangerous and destructive and will appear to us as grotesque. At the same time, our own grave misjudgments about what are righteous practices for ourselves but which in fact are far from blameless, might well appear to another life form as absurd and even evil. Collateral damages to humankind and to the earth stemming from our enterprises and social activities that we consent to as acceptable, may not fit the judgments of another race of beings. Were the two of us actually to meet, we might be judged as malicious, all our assumed self-righteousness to the contrary notwithstanding. We would do well never to show them one of our sci-fi movies.

The creators of most science fiction movies seem to feel that any story line less confrontational and belligerent than they usually portray would never appeal to our extremely competitive and confrontational culture. The whole *Star Trek* series is based on the fictional policing of criminal galactic activities requiring much warfare and destructive efforts similar to our earthbound experiences. Nevertheless, the movies *E.T., Close Encounters of the Third Kind*, and *Cocoon* all depicted relatively peaceful encounters. One cannot but wonder what might be the effect on our culture if a majority of the movies and fiction books were of that genre. We might well be less fearful and our own belligerent attitudes might even be tempered.

While our fictitious images of the universe reflect our roughshod and often brutal ways and values, the actual peaceful cosmic circumstances that may prevail, most surely would have a powerful effect on the formation of more peaceful mindsets for ourselves, provided we are in touch with the actual cosmos and not just our own constructs of it. The universe is the soil of our physical and even spiritual being, and that actual physical cosmos has a more powerful effect on us than any of our imaginations. We are after all part of a vast Creation ecosystem that basically functions according to the mind and intent of a loving Creator.

It is not so important that we come to know precisely the nature of other life forms that may exist, as it is important that we better understand what we could become through constructive relationship to the rest of the universe. If we are open to extraordinary new possibilities, we may not gain detailed facts about that far-flung universe, but our whole Spiritual being including mind and will, may grow from such stimuli and our sense of the Divine Creator could expand. It is all within our purview as an intelligent asset of Creation. We are designed to not only exist and occupy a space within this universe, but are designed to contribute to the ongoing processes of earth and Creation, perhaps like a child contributes something valuable to a family even though it is physically and intellectually powerless; and aged adults are also valuable assets to family and community in spite of diminished potentials. It is our nature as human beings to have relational effects on one another, and would it not also be true of neighboring aliens?

Our best strategy for a secure and fruitful future on this earth is not an overpowering defense plan in preparation for possible damaging confrontations, but explicit anticipation for life enhancing encounters. The God who we have assumed to exist as a community of persons (Father, Son, and Holy Spirit), and in whose image we have been created, and after whom our lives in communal associations have found their basis, has surely designed us for peaceful communion with foreigners. At the same time, for such extraordinary associations to be successful, we need work through some troubling attitudes we have that make earthly associations so unsettling. It seems we have yet fully to accept difficult individual differences among us. Nonetheless, relationships with galactic foreigners would naturally be compatible, being based on the same Divine Creator model. There is probably a basic Creation harmony also based on the Divine model.

It has been suggested that the dangerous aliens depicted in books and movies represent our own dangerous and destructive mental constructs that threaten our well-being and the wellbeing of the earth. Those stories suggest Creation gone off course under the malevolent influence of misused Creator-given gifts that were intended for and are capable of great Creation good. We fear our errant potentials that we transfer onto other possible beings; yet instinctively we also know our created potentials for good, and we do well to build upon these genuine Creator-given gifts.

121

Some say the earth has been visited by extraterrestrial beings over and over again down through history, citing examples of visible activity supposedly unexplainable by human efforts. I take no stance one way or the other on that. However, be that as it may, instead of worrying ourselves into a state of anxiety over such unexplained matters because we fear whoever or whatever is doing these things might be as dangerous as we know ourselves to be, we can help ourselves much more by getting in touch with our created gifts within. If we cannot trust our own human nature, how will we ever trust an alien?

The universe is probably not a hostile place. It all bears the stamp of the Creator. Wherever there is beauty and good, there is the stamp of the Creator. Rather than look for signs of trouble, we do better to look for that stamp of the Creator. We earthlings bear the special stamp of mind and will which means we can be ministers of the munificence of the Creator. We can only guess what kind of Creator gifts might accompany visitors from unfamiliar realms of the universe—perhaps medicinal procedures and chemicals, or improved use of natural elements. For sure, if we expect the worst we will quite likely act accordingly, but collaboration with befriending alien visitors would more likely result in Creation's natural peace. However, if we cannot even imagine it in literature and movies, Creation may continue to be thwarted in its natural tendency to peace and wellbeing. Nonetheless, the authentic human image is deep down within us, perhaps buried under the scars and debris of many millennia of wrong-headedness.

Jesus came among us as a healer for a good reason. Regrettably, we seem to have misinterpreted the full meaning of the life and teachings of Jesus the Messiah. He did not come to raise us above our earthly status but to reinforce our basic earthiness. His Grace builds upon our earthly foundations. His Grace is the very Word of Creation, the Word that made all things good and is now the Word of a New Creation. The Cross, the sign of his vanquishing power over evil has been planted in the soil of the earth, which means it is planted in the bits and pieces of matter assembled here from throughout the universe. The roots of that Cross and the saving effects accomplished on that Cross are growing on the earth, refreshing all Creation.

We are obligated also to carry that Cross on our journey to Salvation, and we are empowered by that Cross with the very energy of Jesus himself. Jesus, the Word of the Creator, by dying on that Cross, spoke the word of renewed life, a New Creation. We the disciples of Jesus, now formed into his Mystical Body, the Church, give flesh to that renewed Creation. That is the basic reality of who we are as Church. We are so much more than just a gathering of folks struggling to live up to obligations, but we are disciples entrusted with new life that brings this life to all Creation. No matter the size or shape of life forms we may encounter one day, we are all creatures of the one Creator, sharing in differing forms of life based on the Creator's own.

We need get beyond the fears of the unknown and live in the known reality of Creation. Faith and science both agree everything in Creation seems to exist to promote life in its many forms. Jesus said he came that we might have life and have it to the fullest, yet we so often reject that full life because we do not recognize it. Full life begins with original Creation life. Either we add to that by our own personal life-enhancing decisions and efforts that promote communal life, or we can subtract from it by conceited self-centeredness that denies shared existence with others on the earth or with those from beyond our earth boundaries. We have awesome potentials in which even visiting aliens would in all likelihood share. Even if we never actually have such encounters with other life forms, and that is more likely than not, might this be the ultimate feature of our stewardship of the earth, becoming ever more welcoming inhabitants of the Creator's earth garden.

Appendix

Psalm 104

Bless the Lord, O my soul!
O Lord, my God, you are great indeed!
You are clothed with majesty and glory,
robed in light as with a cloak.
You have spread out the heavens like a tent-
Cloth;
you have constructed your palace upon
the waters.
You make the clouds your chariot;
you travel on the wings of the wind.
You make the winds your messengers,
and flaming fire your ministers.

You fixed the earth upon its
foundations, not to be moved forever;
With the ocean, as with a garment,
you covered it;
above the mountains the waters stood.
At your rebuke they fled,
at the sound of your thunder they
took to flight;
As the mountains rose, they went
down the valleys
to the place you had fixed for them.
You set a limit they may not pass.
nor shall they cover the earth again.

You send forth springs into the
watercourses
that wind among the mountains,
And give drink to every beast of the
field,
till the wild asses quench their thirst.
Beside them the birds of heaven dwell.
from among the branches they
send forth their song.
You water the mountains from your
palace;

the earth is replete with the fruit
of your works.
You raise grass for the cattle,
and vegetation for men to use,
Producing bread from the earth,
and wine to gladden men's hearts,
So that their faces gleam with oil,
and bread fortifies the hearts
of men.
Well watered are the trees of
the cedars of Lebanon, which
he planted;
In them the birds build their nests;
fir trees are the home of the stork.
The high mountains are for wild goats;
the cliffs are a refuge for
rock-badgers.

You made the moon to mark the
seasons;
the sun knows the hour of its
setting.
You bring darkness, and it is night.
then all the beasts of the forest
roam about;
Young lions roar for the prey
and seek their food from God.
When the sun rises, they withdraw
and crouch in their dens.
Man goes forth to his work,
and to his tillage till the evening.

How manifold are your works,
O Lord!
In wisdom you have wrought them all
The earth is full of your creatures;
The sea also, great and wide,
In which are schools without
Number.
Of living things both small and

Great.
And where the ships move about
with Leviathan, which you formed
to make sport of it

They all look to you
To give them food in due time.
When you give it to them, they
gather it,
when you open your hand, they are
filled with good things.
If you hide your face, they are
dismayed;
If you take away their breath,
they perish
and return to their dust.
When you send forth your spirit, they
are created,
and you renew the face of the earth.

May the glory of the Lord endure
forever;
may the Lord be glad in his work!
He who looks upon the earth, and
it trembles;
who touches the mountains,
and they smoke!
I will sing to the Lord all my life;
I will sing praise to my God while
I live.
Pleasing to him be my theme;
I will be glad in the Lord.
May sinners cease from the earth,
and may the wicked be no more.
Bless the Lord, O my soul!

Song of the Soul
by Kahil Gibran

In depths of my soul there is
A wordless song—a song that lives
In the seed of my heart.
It refuses to melt with ink on
Parchment; it engulfs my affection
In a transparent cloak and flows,
But not upon my lips.

How can I sing it? I fear it may
Mingle with earthly ether;
To whom shall I sing it? It dwells
In the house of my soul in fear of
Harsh ears.

When I look into my inner eyes
I see the shadow of its shadow;
When I touch my fingertips
I feel its vibrations.

The deeds of my hands heed its
Presence as a lake must reflect
The glittering stars; my tears
Reveal it, as bright drops of dew
Reveal the secret of a withering rose.
It is a song composed by contemplation,
And published by silence,
And shunned by clamor,
And folded by truth,
And repeated by dreams,
And understood by love,
And hidden by awakening,
And sung by the soul.
Who dares unite the roar of the sea
And the singing of the nightingale?
Who dares compare the shrieking tempest
To the sigh of an infant?
Who dares speak aloud the words

Fr. Raymond Kirtz O.M.I.

Intended for the heart to speak?
What human dares sing in voice
The song of God